THE
ELIMINATION DIET
COOKBOOK

The ELIMINATION DIET

COOKBOOK

110 Easy, Allergen-Free Recipes to Identify Food Sensitivities

AMANDA FOOTE, RD

PHOTOGRAPHY BY
ELYSA WEITALA

ROCKRIDGE
PRESS

This book is dedicated to my husband, parents, family, friends, and past coworkers who always made sure I had something to eat at every get-together that was free from my allergens.

Interior and Cover Designer: John Calmeyer Art Producer: Meg Baggott Editor: Justin Hartung

Photography © 2020 Elysa Weitala Food styling by Victoria Woollard Author photo courtesy of Brandon Young/ Hardstep Design

ISBN: Print 978-1-64739-022-8 eBook 978-1-64739-023-5 R0

CONTENTS

It is with great pleasure that I welcome you to *The Elimination Diet Cookbook*! This book is filled with easy, tasty recipes that are free of major allergens and customizable to help you identify food sensitivities and adapt to them. Each recipe is quick to prepare and includes easy-to-find ingredients to help keep the process as stress-free as possible. Eliminating 9 major allergens can feel intimidating, but my hope is that this book eases the process for you and fills your plate with delectable meals.

I am uniquely qualified to guide you through this diet because I am a registered dietitian specializing in food allergies and intolerances. I also have them myself and have used the elimination diet several times in my own journey.

I have struggled with food allergies and intolerances my entire life. As an infant, I required nondairy formula. During middle school, I had to run to the bathroom so many times after eating dairy-filled lunches that my guidance counselor assumed I was ill. I started trying to limit dairy during high school, and I got serious about it in college. It was not until my early 20s that I was formally diagnosed with a dairy allergy. But I also had other food reactions, including egg, sesame, and mango. Finally, at 29, I was accurately diagnosed with FPIES (food protein-induced enterocolitis syndrome), a rare form of food allergies that causes severe gastrointestinal distress rather than reactions like difficulty breathing or rashes. My egg, sesame, and mango "allergies" are actually food intolerances and sensitivities.

I fully understand how frustrating it can be to figure out what is going on with your body, especially if you are trying to do it on your own. I became a dietitian after having to teach myself how to eat around my allergies and intolerances. It is my professional and personal mission to help other people navigate food allergies, intolerances, and sensitivities.

This book is meant for anyone who is curious about whether they might have a food intolerance or sensitivity.

It is not intended to diagnose you with a food allergy. If you have been diagnosed with a food allergy or have ever experienced allergic reactions like difficulty breathing, you should consult with your doctor before using this book.

That being said, the 110 recipes in this book are free from the top 8 allergens (milk, egg, wheat, soy, peanut, tree nut, fish, and shellfish) plus sesame (more on that later), so no matter what your situation, you'll find plenty to enjoy. The recipes use common and accessible ingredients for the elimination phase of the diet, and every one includes tips for reintroducing foods. You will also find tools like a comprehensive list of foods to avoid; an easy three-phase process for identifying and eliminating sensitivities, including a sample meal plan to get started; a sample food tracker to help identify problematic triggers when reintroducing foods; and an index of recipes for reintroducing specific allergens.

You do not have to sacrifice tasty and delicious meals on the road to a better and healthier self.

Part One

THE

DIET

Chapter One

THE ELIMINATION DIET

THIS CHAPTER WILL provide you with the basics of the elimination diet: the what, the why, and the how. Embarking on an elimination diet requires foundational knowledge about food allergies, intolerances, and sensitivities; the foods that are the most common suspects; and what you can hope to expect from the diet. The recipes in this book are designed for the elimination phase of the diet, with tips in each recipe for reintroducing common trigger foods to test your body's reaction. This approach allows you to tailor the diet to your exact needs. For example, if you have discovered that wheat is safe for you, you can proceed with the recipes in this book without avoiding wheat.

WHAT IS AN ELIMINATION DIET?

An elimination diet is a tool to identify non-allergic food intolerances and sensitivities. At its core, the diet involves eliminating a food or food group from your diet to see if your health improves and then reintroducing the food in a controlled manner to see if your symptoms return. If your symptoms return, you are intolerant of or sensitive to that food; if they do not, that food may be safe for you to consume but perhaps in smaller amounts. Through this process, you will find the foods that work for your unique body, keeping you feeling your best and minimizing uncomfortable symptoms.

Each person's body is different, and the foods that cause reactions and the reactions themselves are unique. The elimination diet is intended to be used short-term to help identify sensitivity triggers. Identifying one food sensitivity could happen as soon as one week or in up to six to eight weeks. However, on average, if a food bothers you, eliminating it from your diet should yield near-instant results. For example, if you feel ill after eating cheese, and you eliminate dairy from your diet, you should feel better without it.

If you suspect that you have a true food allergy, which can produce dangerous and even life-threatening reactions, the elimination diet and any reintroduction should be done under the direct supervision of a doctor. This book is intended to help you identify food intolerances and sensitivities that are not life-threatening. The difference between allergies, intolerances, and sensitivities will be discussed in detail on page 5.

Completely eliminating a food from your diet and then "challenging" the food by reintroducing it to your diet in a controlled manner is the tried-and-true method for identifying food intolerances and sensitivities. The elimination diet is a tool used by doctors and dietitians to help patients discover their trigger foods. This book will help you make these discoveries on your own, though working with your health care provider can provide additional benefits.

As a patient, I have participated in numerous elimination diets involving common triggers like dairy, egg, and wheat and also less common triggers like tomatoes and potatoes. As a dietitian, I guide my clients through the elimination diet and food reintroduction to diagnose food intolerances and sensitivities and provide them with individualized plans of action. This method is extremely effective and is the gold standard in identifying trigger foods.

FOOD ALLERGIES, INTOLERANCES, AND SENSITIVITIES

While investigating potential dietary restrictions you may have seen different terms being used interchangeably. Food allergies, intolerances, and sensitivities are actually different, and knowing the difference can be helpful. Each condition is defined in the following section, and despite their differences, an elimination diet can help with each.

FOOD ALLERGIES

A food allergy is an abnormal immune reaction to the proteins in a food. In other words, when that food is eaten or touched, the immune system overreacts as if the food is a harmful substance that is a danger to the body. Over 10 percent of the American population has a food allergy. Food allergies are classified as IgE-mediated, non-IgE-mediated, or a combination.

IgE-mediated food allergies, in which IgE allergy antibodies in the body cause the allergic reaction, are the most common and most commonly discussed. They result in immediate symptoms such as anaphylaxis (rapid systemic reaction causing respiratory and cardiovascular distress); oral allergy syndrome (swelling or discomfort in the mouth); hives, rashes, or lesions; or immediate gastrointestinal distress such as vomiting. These food allergies are diagnosed through blood or skin testing. People with these food allergies always need to carry epinephrine with them and take extreme precautions to avoid the food. Some food allergies can be outgrown, but they are completely individual to each person and outgrowing them is not guaranteed. Some people may be able to undergo oral immunotherapy to build tolerance to the food.

Non-IgE-mediated food allergies, in which the allergic reaction is caused by something different in the body than IgE antibodies, are rare and less understood even to the medical community. The symptoms are delayed, sometimes for hours, causing severe vomiting and diarrhea that can lead to severe dehydration and systemic shock or contact dermatitis. This condition is called FPIES (food protein-induced enterocolitis syndrome) and can be life-threatening. People with FPIES may need to carry anti-emetic medication (which prevents vomiting) and take extreme precautions to avoid the triggering food. Most infants and children with FPIES will outgrow the condition, but it is possible that it persists well into adulthood.

Combined food allergies are caused by IgE antibodies and other cells in the body, resulting in atopic dermatitis (autoimmune response), eosinophilic esophagitis (difficulty eating, reflux, choking, and vomiting), or eosinophilic gastroenteritis (fluid buildup in the abdomen, swelling, or obstruction in the digestive system). It is uncommon to outgrow these food allergies.

If you suspect that you have a food allergy, do not use this book as a diagnostic tool. Consult with your doctor and work with them to use this book as a resource for safe recipes because all 110 recipes are free of the top 9 allergens.

FOOD INTOLERANCES

A food intolerance is the inability to properly digest a food, which can cause uncomfortable symptoms like bloating, cramping, nausea, reflux, diarrhea, headache, fatigue, or rashes. Over 20 percent of the world population has at least one food intolerance.

The most known food intolerance is lactose intolerance, caused by a biological lack of the enzyme lactase in the gut, which helps digest lactose. A surprising majority of adults are lactose intolerant to some degree, inspiring products on the market such as lactase enzyme in pill or tablet form to help people eat dairy-containing foods with fewer symptoms.

Symptoms of a food intolerance usually occur within a few hours of eating the food, and the condition is not life-threatening. Food intolerances are unique to the individual, and it might take only a few bites of the food to cause symptoms, or it might take frequent intake or a large portion of the food to cause symptoms.

Despite food intolerances not being life-threatening, it is still important to avoid the triggering food to prevent your body from undergoing frequent stress and inflammation. Because your body does not create the enzymes required to digest that food, you are unlikely to outgrow an intolerance toward it.

FOOD SENSITIVITIES

A food sensitivity differs from both food allergies and intolerances in that it is unrelated to the immune system or digestion of the food. You might find that after eating a certain food, you just don't feel quite right. You might have some mental "fogginess," fatigue, body pain, or general feeling of malaise. These symptoms may indicate you are sensitive to a food. It is unclear how many people have food sensitivities, but it is possible that anyone could feel unwell after eating particular foods, a feeling completely unique to their own body. Food sensitivities may come and go throughout your life, depending on your phase of life and current situation.

For the purposes of this book, the terms *food intolerances* and *sensitivities* are interchangeable and will be referred to as *intolerance*.

THE TOP 8 ALLERGENS
(Plus One Extra)

Though this book is intended for food intolerances, the top 9 food allergens are the focus of the elimination diet, since they are the most common trigger foods. The top 8 food allergens (commonly referred to as the "top 8" or "big 8") are milk, eggs, wheat, soy, tree nut, peanut, fish, and shellfish.

Milk: Some obvious sources of milk include liquid milk, heavy cream, coffee creamer, sour cream, cream cheese, cheese, yogurt, and ice cream. Milk is hidden in countless foods, such as baked goods, packaged goods like cookies and crackers, flavorings on chips, spice blends, candy, breaded items, granola bars, canned soups, salad dressings, and even frozen French fries. The presence of milk may not be obvious in many foods, so read the ingredient lists for words like *whey*, *casein*, *caseinates*, *lactose*, *lactulose*, *milk*, *butter*, *cheese*, *yogurt*, and *curds*. If you find that you are intolerant of milk products, it is important to get nutrients such as calcium, vitamin D, protein, and vitamin B_2 elsewhere.

Eggs: Though you may be thinking of just avoiding scrambled eggs for breakfast or mayonnaise on your sandwich, eggs are also hidden in many baked goods, pastas, ice cream, nougat, and even marshmallows. Words to look for include *albumin*, *egg solids*, *egg wash*, *meringue*, *ovalbumin*, *powdered egg*, and *lecithin*. If avoiding eggs, find other sources to get your choline, omega-3s, protein, vitamin D, selenium, and lutein.

Wheat: When you think of troubles with wheat, you might automatically assume celiac disease is the culprit. Celiac disease is an autoimmune disease that involves serious damage to the small intestines whenever gluten is consumed. It is possible to have a wheat or gluten intolerance even if you do not have celiac disease. Wheat and other gluten-containing grains are commonly used in baked goods, pastas, tortillas, cereals, pancakes, and waffles. Less obvious sources of gluten include beer and other alcohols, malt, and soy sauce.

Soy: One of the trickiest foods to avoid on an elimination diet is soy. It seems these days that soy is used in just about everything. There is not just edamame, tofu, and soy milk to consider. Soy comes in many forms, such as flour, bran, concentrate, fiber, protein, paste, and sauces. Foods that contain soy include soy milk, soy sauce, tamari, tempeh, teriyaki sauce, textured vegetable proteins (commonly used in vegan foods), and artificial flavoring.

Tree Nut and Peanut: Most reactions to nuts are true allergies or oral allergy syndrome, but it is possible to have a nut intolerance. Tree nuts include nuts such as almonds, cashews, pistachios, walnuts, pecans, macadamia nuts, pine nuts, Brazil nuts, chestnuts, hazelnuts, and hickory nuts. Whole nuts, nut butters, nut milks, nut flours, and nut extracts are sold separately and are commonly used in many products. Nuts are often hidden in baked goods, ice cream, candy, cereal, granola, trail mix, energy bars, salad dressings, and sauces.

Fish and Shellfish: A seafood intolerance can come from finfish like salmon, tuna, tilapia, and trout; from crustaceans like crab, lobster, shrimp, crawfish, and prawns; or from mollusks like scallops and oysters. You may find that you tolerate finfish fine, but not crustaceans, or that you can tolerate one finfish like salmon, but not another like sardines. Every stomach is unique, so just because one fish bothers you, another may be perfectly fine to include in your diet. Hidden sources of seafood include fish oil, Worcestershire sauce, imitation crab, sushi, and ceviche. If eliminating seafood from your diet, be sure to get your omega-3 fatty acids from other sources.

In addition to the top 8 allergens, a person can be allergic to any food. For example, common FPIES food allergens include oats, rice, chicken, turkey, and peas. Other common food allergies include sesame seeds, corn, mustard, strawberries, bananas, and even spices. As of 2019, sesame seeds are the ninth most prevalent food allergen, and as such, all recipes in this book are also sesame-free.

BENEFITS OF THE ELIMINATION DIET

The elimination diet is a diagnostic tool, and although the diet is short lived, the benefits of the diet are lifelong. Imagine going through an entire day, week, or month with no uncomfortable symptoms. It may be hard to imagine now, depending on how much you are suffering, but it is completely possible. Long term, completing this diet will set you on a path of eating a diet of foods that nourish, not irritate, your body.

It may feel counterintuitive that restricting your diet could reduce (not create) stress, but knowledge is power. Instead of being leery of the food you order at a restaurant, you can feel confident in ordering your meal without your trigger foods (i.e., no cheese, please) and enjoy your food again without fearing unpleasant consequences.

Once you get started on the elimination diet, here are 10 ways it can help you:

- Identifying your trigger foods
- Possibly reducing symptoms of irritable bowel syndrome (IBS)
- Reducing bloating and gas
- Reducing stomach pain and cramping
- Reducing constipation
- Reducing diarrhea
- Possibly reducing fatigue and mental fog
- Possibly improving sleep
- Possibly improving skin condition, such as reducing eczema
- Possibly reducing chronic migraines

I cannot even express how much better I felt when I identified my trigger foods and eliminated them from my diet. With no exaggeration, I felt like a new person. I felt healthier, happier, less stressed, more confident in my dietary choices, empowered, and relieved.

Seven Tips for a Healthier You

You can, without a doubt, do this. Eliminating nine major catego-ries of food is a large undertaking, but don't be intimidated; it is simpler than you might fear. Some simple tips will help you get through the process.

1. **Be prepared.** Set yourself up for success by organizing your kitchen, planning your meals, and making shopping lists.

2. **Be open.** Temporarily letting go of your eating habits and eliminating large food groups may feel intimidating, but try to be open to the process. The light at the end of the tunnel is a healthier, happier you. I think that is worth the effort!

3. **Be patient.** You may not feel better right away; it may take time to notice benefits from the elimination phase. It may be tempting to eat an off-limits food, but if you do, you will have to start the diet over.

4. **Embrace variety.** This cookbook does not include any obscure ingredients, but keeping an open mind to a new eating pat-tern, new culinary styles, and new flavor profiles will help you embrace the diet. Plan your weekly meals with a variety of flavors to keep the diet exciting.

5. **Stay hydrated.** Most of us do not drink enough water as it is, and when making such drastic changes to your diet, water is your biggest ally. Adequate hydration keeps your entire body working in tip-top condition and can help reduce any dis-comfort when changing your diet. Also, often, feeling hungry may be thirst in disguise, so if you find yourself wanting to munch on forbidden snacks, have a glass of water instead!

6. **Be honest.** Transparency with your friends and family will help you stay accountable on the diet and allows them to be a part of your team. The people around you are a great resource for positivity and encouragement.

7. **Eat enough.** Because this diet greatly limits the packaged goods and convenience foods available to you, try to plan your meals and snacks and eat regularly to prevent yourself from getting too hungry to the point where you might want to reach for whatever is closest, even if it is not allowed on the diet.

To ensure proper nutrition when permanently eliminating entire groupings of food from your diet, a registered dietitian is your best resource. For example, if you permanently eliminate dairy, you may need to find other sources to get adequate calcium and vitamin D. These food sources are not always obvious, and a dietitian can help round out your diet. The recipes in this book are a great start to teaching you how to eat a well-rounded diet without trigger foods.

Chapter Two

ELIMINATION DIET PHASES

IT IS TIME to get to the heart of the diet: what to do. You will be entering into a three-phase process: planning, elimination, and reintroduction. Planning will get you on the right track, making the diet stress-free. During elimination, you will be eating meals completely free from the trigger foods you are testing for. During reintroduction, you will be reintroducing one food at a time to see how your body reacts. For example, after completely avoiding milk, you will reintroduce it in a controlled manner to see how you feel.

PHASE ONE: **PLANNING**

This diet does require some planning, but it is quite simple. With some positive thinking, support persons, note-taking, label reading, and meal planning, you will be prepared and ready to start feeling better. Elimination requires complete adherence, so for this short period of time, no cheating is allowed; this discipline will help you achieve the best outcomes while on the diet.

MINDFUL PREPARATION

The elimination diet can seem overwhelming, but with some simple tips, you can prepare yourself for this adventure, and these recipes will ensure that you will still enjoy your food. The first step is to remind yourself that this is temporary. This diet is a tool to learn how foods affect your body, and once you learn that, you will come out the other side feeling better and knowing what foods are best for you.

The second step is to keep a journal or food diary (page 177) to help track your reactions. This will go a long way toward reducing stress and guesswork. When you look back at your journal entries, you will be able to identify patterns. For example, you eliminated milk and soy, and when you reintroduced soy, you felt fine, but when you reintroduced milk, your symptoms returned.

MEAL PLANNING AND YOUR KITCHEN

While you begin the elimination diet, your pantry and refrigerator may need a mini makeover. The simplest and most practical solution is to reserve a shelf or drawer in your refrigerator, freezer, and pantry for your new "safe" foods. There is no reason to throw away perfectly good food that you may not be intolerant to.

Begin by reading the labels of the foods you already have, and if they contain even one of the top 9 (milk, egg, tree nut, peanut, shellfish, wheat, soy, fish, or sesame) that you are avoiding, clear it off your new safe shelf.

For the elimination diet, the foods that are not free of the ingredients you are avoiding are off limits, but don't worry. As you discover what foods you can tolerate, you can reintroduce these products.

Make yourself a weekly meal plan from the recipes in this book for breakfast, lunch, dinner, and snacks so you know exactly what to shop for. You will follow this process during reintroduction by making your shopping list include the foods you plan on reintroducing, which are outlined in each recipe.

The easiest way to shop for this diet is to shop for whole foods in their most natural form, such as whole fruits, vegetables, meats, and grains, and avoid purchasing prepackaged foods as much as possible. Prepackaged foods are likely to contain one or several of the top 9. Unless a recipe specifically calls for a packaged ingredient (like gluten-free pasta), you will be using whole foods in this cookbook. The recipes use simple cooking methods and equipment you are likely to have in your kitchen, such as pots and pans, baking sheets, and microwave-safe bowls.

THE RIGHT SUPPORT

Living with dietary restrictions can feel overwhelming and lonely. Feeling like you cannot eat the same foods as your friends or family, having to check the menu before you go out, and asking to speak to the manager are examples of how food intolerance affects more than just your health. Surrounding yourself with supportive, caring people makes all the difference. Family, friends, and even social media are great resources to have in your corner during the elimination diet and while moving forward into your newfound dietary restrictions. Simply explain to those close to you that you are embarking on this journey to improve your health and that their support is immensely helpful. Online platforms like Facebook and Instagram have become homes to some of the largest support groups online. A simple search will lead you straight to people with the same restrictions and endless tips, recipes, and product recommendations.

PHASE TWO: **ELIMINATION**

The elimination diet does not require you to remove all top 9 foods from your diet, only the ones you wish to check for sensitivities. You can do this in one of two ways, whichever you feel makes more sense for your situation.

1. Eliminate all the foods you are checking for sensitivities, and reintroduce one food at a time while still avoiding the other foods. For example: eliminate milk, egg, and wheat, then reintroduce milk while still eliminating egg and wheat.

2. Eliminate one food you are checking for sensitivities, reintroduce that food, then repeat the process for all other foods you wish to test. For example, eliminate milk, then reintroduce milk; eliminate eggs, then reintroduce eggs.

Regardless of the method you choose, the elimination phase should last a minimum of two weeks. The standard for elimination diets is four to eight weeks of complete elimination, which is a huge time commitment, especially if you choose to test each food separately with its own elimination and reintroduction phases. Anything shorter than two weeks and you will not get a true sense of how your body felt without the food. Two weeks is a good starting point because 14 days will fly by, and in less than half a month, you will be ready to get life-changing answers to your diet.

The work you do in the planning phase will help you put a successful plan into action during the elimination phase, which can be challenging but achievable. Use the meal plan (page 25) to help get you started on identifying potential sensitivities.

FOODS YOU CAN EAT

So far you might be focusing heavily on all the foods you cannot eat, but the good news is that you can still eat most foods. The challenge is that you can only eat foods that you prepare, rather than eating from a to-go bag or cellophane package.

The foods listed here are those with a very low likelihood of triggering any reactions. The recipes in part 2 make use of these safe ingredients.

MILK ALTERNATIVES

Hemp milk	Pea milk	Rice milk

MEATS

Beef	Lamb	Turkey
Chicken	Pork	Wild game

GRAINS AND STARCHES

Brown rice	Oats	Wild rice
Corn *(corn chips, corn tortillas, popcorn)*	Quinoa	*(breads, pastas, and other products made from these ingredients)*
	White rice	

FATS

Avocado and avocado oil

Canola oil

Coconut oil

Corn oil

Dairy-free and soy-free buttery spreads like Earth Balance®

Olive oil

(Coconuts are botanically a fruit, not a nut; although coconut is not used in this book, you may use the recipes to test for a coconut intolerance.)

FRUITS AND VEGETABLES

Apples

Apricots

Asparagus

Avocados

Bananas

Beets

Blueberries

Broccoli

Brussels sprouts

Cabbage

Celery

Cherries

Chiles

Corn

Cucumbers

Grapefruit

Grapes

Kale

Kiwis

Lemons

Lettuce

Limes

Mangos

Melons

Mushrooms

Onions

Oranges

Papayas

Peaches

Pears

Peas

Peppers

Pineapples

Plums

Potatoes

Raspberries

Spinach

Squash

Strawberries

Sweet potatoes

Tomatoes

Yams

Zucchini

(every fruit and vegetable!)

BEANS AND LEGUMES

Black beans

Chickpeas

Green beans

Kidney beans

Lentils

Lima beans

Navy beans

Peas

Pinto beans

White beans

Chia	Poppy	Sunflower and sun butter
Flax	Pumpkin	
Hemp		

OTHER

Dairy- and soy-free chocolate	Pepper	Sugar
Herbs	Salt	Vinegar
Honey	Spices	

Smoothies and Other Drinks to Enjoy

Because fruits and vegetables are all safe ingredients on the elimination diet, smoothies are a quick and easy staple and a simple source of maximum nutrition. Delicious, refreshing, and easily customizable, smoothies are covered in the breakfast chapter. Luckily, almost all drinks are available to you on the elimination diet. Water, black coffee (without creamer or flavoring), tea, fruit juice, sparkling water, carbonated beverages, vegetable juice, and rice milk are all great choices when reaching for a drink.

Please note that many alcohols contain top 9 ingredients. Beer and malt beverages are wheat-based and often contain nuts for flavoring. Wine may contain milk, eggs, and even fish products during the refining process. Gin and vermouth may contain nuts. Vodka is primarily made from potatoes but can also be made from wheat or soy and can contain nut flavorings. Whiskey, Scotch, and bourbon are often made from wheat and may contain nuts. Rum commonly contains milk or nut products for flavoring.

FOODS TO AVOID

You will be avoiding all processed, packaged, and convenience foods during the elimination phase of the diet. These items are highly likely to contain the top 9 foods or to have come into contact with them. Because of the likelihood that alcohol contains the top 9, you will also be abstaining from alcohol. Although this book uses no coffee or tea, you may choose to eliminate caffeine because it can also cause stomach upset.

MILK

Baked goods that contain milk (breads, cookies, cakes, bagels, muffins, English muffins, donuts, crackers, brownies)

Breaded foods like fried chicken

Candy that contains milk

Canned soups

Cheese of any sort (Cheddar, mozzarella, Swiss, parmesan, etc.)

Chip dips like queso, ranch, and French onion

Coffee creamer, liquid or powdered

Cream cheese

Custard

Dried milk

Flavored chips, crackers, pretzels

Granola bars that contain milk

Heavy cream

Ice cream

Instant milk

Frozen treats like ice cream sandwiches

Liquid milk

Milk-based salad dressings like ranch, Caesar, blue cheese

Protein bars

Protein powder

Pudding

Sour cream

Yogurt

EGGS

Baked goods that contain egg (breads, cookies, cakes, bagels, muffins, English muffins, donuts, brownies)

Custard

Eggs, whole

Egg noodles

Egg powder

Egg replacer

Egg substitutes

Egg wash (like on bagels or pretzels)

Egg whites

Egg yolks

French toast

Hollandaise

Ice cream (often made with egg)

Imitation crab/surimi

Macaroni

Marshmallows that contain egg

Marzipan

Mayonnaise

Mayonnaise-based
sauces (Thousand
Island, tartar sauce, aïoli,
remoulade, onion dip)

Meringue

Miracle Whip

Nougat

Pasta made with egg

Pudding

Salad dressing

Soufflé

TREE NUT, PEANUT, AND SESAME

Almonds

Almond butter

Almond flour

Almond meal

Almond milk

Almond paste

Baked goods that
contain nuts

Baklava

Brazil nuts

Cashews

Cashew butter

Cashew milk

Chestnuts

Chestnut flour

Chocolate-hazelnut
spread

Everything
bagel seasoning

Granola

Granola bars

Hazelnuts

Hazelnut flour

Hickory nuts

Hummus

Macadamia nuts

Macadamia nut flour

Macadamia nut milk

Macarons

Marzipan

Nougat

Nut brittle

Nut cheeses

Nut-flavored coffee

Nut liqueur

Nut-milk ice cream

Nut-milk yogurt

Peanuts

Peanut butter

Peanut
butter–flavored candy

Peanut flour

Pecans

Pecan meal

Pesto

Pine nuts

Pistachios

Pistachio flour

Praline

Sesamol

Sesamolin

Tahini

Trail mix

Walnuts

Walnut flour

FISH AND SHELLFISH

Caesar dressing
(with anchovies)

Caviar

Ceviche

Crustaceans
*(crab, crawfish/crayfish,
langoustine, lobster,
prawns, shrimp)*

Finfish
*(anchovies, bass, catfish,
cod, eel, flounder/fluke,
grouper, halibut, herring,
mackerel, mahi-mahi,
pollock, roughy, salmon,
sardine, snapper, sole,
swordfish, tilapia, tuna,
trout, wahoo)*

Fish oil

Fish sauce

Fish sticks

Imitation crab/surimi

Mollusks
*(clams, mussels,
octopus, oysters,
scallops, squid)*

Omega-3 supplements

Sushi

Worcestershire sauce

WHEAT

Ale

Beer

Baked goods
*(bread, muffins,
pancakes, waffles)*

Battered/breaded foods

Bread crumbs

Bulgur

Cereals

Couscous

Crackers

Cracker meal

Cream of wheat

Durum

Farina

Farro

Flour
*(all-purpose, baking,
bleached, bread, cake,
enriched, graham,
instant, pastry,
self-rising, semolina,
sprouted, unbleached,
whole-wheat)*

Flour tortillas

Hot dogs

Imitation crab

Matzoh

Pasta

Seitan

Soy sauce

Wheat bran

Wheat durum

Wheat germ

Wheatgrass

Wheat malt

Wheat sprouts

Wheat starch

Worcestershire sauce

SOY

Any product with soy on the ingredients label *(It is hidden in countless products.)*	Soy cheese	Soy sauce
	Soy concentrate	Soy sprouts
	Soy curds	Soy yogurt
Edamame	Soy fiber	Tamari
Miso	Soy flour	Tempeh
Natto	Soy ice cream	Teriyaki sauce
Protein powder	Soy milk	Textured vegetable proteins
Soybeans	Soy nuts	
Soybean oil	Soy paste	Tofu
Soy bran	Soy protein	Worcestershire sauce

PHASE THREE: **REINTRODUCTION**

Once you have completed the elimination phase of the diet, you are ready to begin reintroducing foods to assess your body's reactions. If you have chosen to eliminate the top 9, it is time to reintroduce one food group at a time (for example, add milk but not the other foods of the top 9). If you have chosen to eliminate one food at a time, now is the time to reintroduce that food, and once you have determined your reaction, you will repeat the elimination process with another food.

HOW TO REINTRODUCE FOODS

The only way to see if a food bothers your system is to reintroduce it to your diet. You will reintroduce each food individually every two to three days to assess your reaction. This is simply because if you reintroduce two food groups at once, and you have a bad reaction, it is impossible to tell which food gave you the reaction when the other could be safe.

For example, after eliminating dairy for two weeks, you will reintroduce dairy-containing foods in increasing amounts throughout the day and assess reactions. For example: spread butter on the Light 'n' Fluffy Pancakes (page 44) for breakfast, add cheese and ranch dressing to the Kale Chopped Salad (page 63) for lunch, add cheese and sour cream to the Beef Enchilada Casserole (page 132) for dinner, and make the Peach Sorbet (page 160) with ice cream instead of ice for dessert. Each recipe in this book includes reintroduction tips to take the guesswork out of reintroduction for you. If you are extremely sensitive to dairy, you could be feeling reactions after breakfast, which may be answer enough for you, so you do not have to make yourself suffer through more dairy-filled meals. If you feel fine after breakfast, proceed through lunch and dinner, listening to your body for reactions. It may take up to three days for a reaction to occur, so do not move on to reintroducing the next food group for at least three days. Rather, you'll go back to eating the elimination phase recipes. The Sample 4-Day Dairy Reintroduction Plan (page 33) will give you an idea of how to organize your reintroduction phase.

Note: If you experience any reactions such as shortness of breath, tight throat or chest, oral swelling, change in consciousness, severe vomiting or dehydration, or widespread hives, you should see a doctor or go to the hospital.

MAKING REINTRODUCTION WORK

Reintroduction of food groups may cause uncomfortable symptoms, and although this process is unpleasant, it is information. Imagine knowing without a doubt that sour cream upsets your stomach, but a slice of Swiss cheese is safe. (Swiss cheese is a dairy food that is low in lactose, so many people who are lactose intolerant can tolerate certain hard cheeses like Swiss and parmesan.)

This book includes a handy Sample Food Tracker on page 177 that will make reintroduction easy to manage. Your meal plan will give you a big leg up on organizing for the reintroduction phase. Use the Sample Food Tracker to indicate what foods you are reintroducing, what types (such as milk or cheese), what your reaction is (such as gas), and when the reaction happens (such as two hours after eating).

Achieving success during the reintroduction phase is going to give you so much information moving forward in your life. These five tips will make the process even smoother.

1. **Listen to your body.** You want to see if these foods cause you any discomfort. Listening to our bodies is often drowned out by the noise of stress, rushing around, and obligations. Take the time to quiet your mind and check in with your body: Do you have heartburn or a stomach-ache? Have your bowel movements changed? Have you been missing your daily headache?

2. **Take good notes.** Tracking all your meals and reactions is a lot of work, which is why taking good notes will be your best ally. Using a food tracker (example on page 177) will be a big help.

3. **Be positive.** Trust the process since it is used as the gold standard of diagnosing food intolerances. Even if you experience uncomfortable symptoms, you know you will never have to experience them again!

4. **Even little things matter.** This goes back to listening to your body. You might notice that you wake up easier in the mornings or that your complexion has cleared a bit; these improvements matter and give you more information about which foods might have been causing invisible problems.

5. **If results are unclear, try again.** Some food intolerances take a larger quantity of food ingested to trigger a reaction. Maybe a cheeseburger does not bother you, but if you also dip your fries in ranch and chase it with a milkshake, you are in a world of hurt. If you still suspect that a food bothers you and the reintroduction phase did not trigger a reaction, try reintroducing the food again.

MEAL PLAN

The following meal plan is an example of a 14-day elimination plan. You should use this plan in advance of any allergen reintroduction. Swap in different recipes from the book to suit your preference—they're all free of the top 9 allergens.

	Breakfast	Lunch	Dinner	Snacks and Treats
DAY 1	Blueberry Crumble *(page 45)*	Fancy Ramen *(page 85)*	Baked Chicken Wings *(page 107)*	Veggie Chips *(page 161)*
DAY 2	Sunflower Seed Butter and Banana Smoothie *(page 43)*	Antipasto Salad *(page 62)*	Sweet-and-Sour Pork *(page 126)*	Oatmeal Cookies *(page 167)*
DAY 3	Leftovers Turned Hash *(page 55)*	Avocado-Chicken Salad *(page 70)*	Steak, Peppers, and Onions *(page 137)*	Savory Cereal Mix *(page 169)*
DAY 4	Crispy Vegetable Fritters *(page 52)*	Falafel *(page 103)*	Turkey Burgers *(page 116)*	Popcorn with Flavor Mix-Ins *(page 162)*
DAY 5	Tropical Explosion Smoothie *(page 40)*	Buddha Bowl *(page 68)*	Chicken Lo Mein *(page 117)*	Sunflower Seed Butter and Chocolate Cereal Mix *(page 170)*
DAY 6	Steel-Cut Oatmeal *(page 46)*	Taco Salad *(page 74)*	Yellow Curried Potatoes *(page 102)*	Candied Dried Fruit *(page 164)*
DAY 7	Zucchini Bread *(page 49)*	Kalamata Chicken Bowl *(page 75)*	Mini Meatloaves *(page 134)*	Crispy Rice Cereal Treats *(page 165)*

SHOPPING LIST FOR WEEK 1
OF ELIMINATION PHASE

PRODUCE

- Arugula (1 bunch)
- Avocados (3)
- Bananas (4)
- Beets (1 pound)
- Bell pepper, any color (1)
- Bell pepper, orange (1)
- Bell pepper, red, orange, or yellow (1)
- Bell pepper, yellow (1)
- Bell peppers, green (2)
- Bell peppers, red (2)
- Blueberries (3 pints)
- Broccoli (2 heads)
- Cabbage (1 head)
- Carrots (6)
- Carrots, baby (12 ounces)
- Cauliflower (1 head)
- Fruit, any kind, sliced (½ cup)

- Leafy greens, your choice (2 [5-ounce] bags)
- Limes (2)
- Mushrooms, button (8 ounces)
- Mushrooms, shiitake (2 ounces)
- Onion, red (1)
- Onions, white (2)
- Onions, yellow (2)
- Parsley (2 bunches)
- Potatoes, white (2 pounds)
- Potatoes, Yukon Gold (2 pounds)
- Scallions (1 bunch)
- Spinach (1 bunch)
- Spinach, baby (5 ounces)
- Sweet potatoes (2 pounds)
- Tomatoes, large (2)
- Zucchini (2)

MEAT

- Beef, ground, lean (1½ pounds)
- Beef, steak, flank (1 pound)

- Chicken, breasts, boneless, skinless (2 pounds)

- Chicken, precooked, shredded (1 cup)

- Chicken, wings (1 pound)

- Pork, tenderloin (1 pound)

- Turkey, ground, lean (1 pound)

CANNED AND BOTTLED ITEMS

- Applesauce, unsweetened (1 [24-ounce] jar)

- Beans, black (1 [15-ounce] can)

- Chickpeas (3 [15-ounce] cans)

- Corn (1 [15-ounce] can)

- Garlic, minced (1 [8-ounce] jar)

- Juice, lemon (1 [7-ounce] bottle)

- Olives, black, sliced (1 [4.25-ounce] can)

- Olives, black, whole, pitted (1 [6-ounce] can)

- Olives, green, whole, pitted (1 [5½-ounce] jar)

- Olives, Kalamata, sliced (1 [5.6-ounce] jar)

- Olives, Kalamata, whole, pitted (1 [6-ounce] jar)

- Peas, green (1 [15-ounce] can)

- Peperoncini, sliced, pickled (1 [7¾-ounce] jar)

- Pineapple, chunks (2 [14-ounce] cans)

- Rice milk, plain, unsweetened (1 [32-ounce] container)

- Roasted red peppers (1 [12-ounce] jar)

- Stock, beef, chicken, or vegetable (1 [32-ounce] container)

- Stock, chicken (1 [32-ounce] container)

- Stock, vegetable (1 [32-ounce] container)

- Sun-dried tomatoes (½ cup)

FROZEN FOODS

- Mangos, chunks, frozen (1 pound)

- Peaches, chunks, frozen (1 pound)

- Baking powder
- Baking soda
- Basil, dried
- Brown rice ramen cakes
- Buns, hamburger, gluten-free (4)
- Cereal, corn, square
- Cereal, dry gluten-free
- Cereal, rice, square
- Chili powder
- Chives, dried
- Cinnamon, ground
- Cocoa powder, unsweetened
- Cornstarch
- Cumin, ground
- Curry powder
- Dill weed, dried
- Dried fruit
- Flour, gluten-free, 1-to-1
- Garlic powder
- Ginger, ground
- Honey
- Italian seasoning
- Ketchup
- Marshmallows
- Oats, rolled

- Oats, steel-cut
- Oil, canola
- Oil, olive
- Onion powder
- Oregano, dried
- Paprika
- Pasta, gluten-free, quinoa, chickpea, or lentil spaghetti
- Pepper, cayenne, ground
- Pepper, red, flakes
- Pepper, red, ground
- Peppercorns, black
- Popcorn kernels
- Rice, brown
- Rice, white
- Rosemary, dried
- Salt, table
- Sugar, brown, light or dark
- Sugar, granulated
- Sugar, powdered
- Sunflower seed butter
- Turmeric, ground
- Vanilla extract
- Vinegar, white-wine

	Breakfast	Lunch	Dinner	Snacks and Treats
DAY 8	You'd Never Believe It's a Veggie Smoothie *(page 42)*	Pineapple Barbecue Bowl *(page 78)*	Broccoli, Chicken, and Rice *(page 122)*	Roasted Chickpeas *(page 173)*
DAY 9	Cinnamon Crunch Muffins *(page 47)*	Apple "Pecan" Salad *(page 61)*	Chicken Tikka Masala *(page 112)*	No-Bake Chocolate Bites *(page 171)*
DAY 10	Savory Potato Pancakes *(page 53)*	Chicken Cobb Salad *(page 72)*	One-Pan Meatballs *(page 131)* with Stuffed Mushrooms *(page 153)*	Veggie Chips *(page 161)*
DAY 11	Tater Tot Casserole *(page 56)*	Herbed Cucumber Salad *(page 60)*	Pork Carnitas *(page 127)* with Guacamole and Salsa *(page 172)*	Peach Sorbet *(page 160)*
DAY 12	Tropical Explosion Smoothie *(page 40)*	Spicy Rice Bowl *(page 76)*	Cauliflower Tacos *(page 100)*	Your Favorite Cereal Bars *(page 166)*
DAY 13	Blueberry Crumble *(page 45)*	Fresh California Bowl *(page 64)*	Red Beans and Rice *(page 104)*	Sunflower Seed Butter Cups *(page 175)*
DAY 14	Leftovers Turned Hash *(page 55)*	Southwest Salad *(page 65)*	Peanut-Free Chicken Pad Thai *(page 120)*	Popcorn with Flavor Mix-Ins *(page 162)*

SHOPPING LIST FOR WEEK 2
OF ELIMINATION PHASE

PRODUCE

- Apple, Granny Smith (1)
- Avocados (5)
- Bananas (2)
- Beets (1 pound)
- Bell pepper, any color (2)
- Bell pepper, green (1)
- Bell pepper, red (1)
- Blueberries (3 pints)
- Broccoli (1 crown)
- Cabbage, red (1 head)
- Carrots, baby (12 ounces)
- Cauliflower (1 head)
- Celery (1 bunch)
- Cilantro (2 bunches)
- Cucumbers (2)
- Dill (1 bunch)
- Jalapeño (1)
- Leafy greens, your choice (2 [5-ounce] bags)
- Lettuce, iceberg (1 head)

- Limes (6)
- Mushrooms, cremini (4 ounces)
- Mushrooms, portabella (4)
- Onion, red (1)
- Onions, white (2)
- Onions, yellow (4)
- Parsley (1 bunch)
- Peach (1)
- Pear (1)
- Potatoes, white (3 pounds)
- Scallions (1 bunch)
- Spinach (1 bunch)
- Sweet potatoes (1 pound)
- Tomatoes, cherry or grape (½ pint)
- Tomatoes, large (4)
- Zucchini (1)

MEAT

- Beef, ground, lean (2 pounds)

- Chicken, breasts, boneless, skinless (3½ pounds)

- Chicken, thighs, boneless, skinless (1 pound)

- Pork, boneless roast (1 pound)

- Pork, boneless shoulder (2 pounds)

CANNED AND BOTTLED ITEMS

- Beans, black (1 [15-ounce] can)

- Beans, pinto (1 [15-ounce] can)

- Chickpeas (1 [15-ounce] can)

- Corn (1 [15-ounce] can)

- Diced tomatoes and green chiles (1 [15-ounce] can)

- Garlic, minced (1 [8-ounce] jar)

- Green chile sauce, gluten-free (1 [16-ounce] can)

- Juice, lemon (1 [7-ounce] bottle)

- Juice, orange (2 [16-ounce] bottles)

- Pineapple, chunks (3 [14-ounce] cans)

- Rice milk, plain, unsweetened (1 [32-ounce] container)

- Roasted red peppers (1 [12-ounce] jar)

- Stock, beef (1 [32-ounce] container)

- Stock, vegetable (1 [32-ounce] container)

- Sun-dried tomatoes (2 tablespoons)

- Tomato sauce (2 [15-ounce] cans)

FROZEN FOODS

- Mangos, chunks, frozen (1 pound)

- Peaches, chunks, frozen (2 pounds)

- Spinach, frozen (1 [10-ounce] block)

- Tater tots, frozen (1 pound)

- Baking powder
- Baking soda
- Basil, dried
- Bay leaves
- Beans, red, dried
- Cereal, dry, gluten-free
- Chili paste
- Chili powder
- Chives, dried
- Chocolate chips, dark, 60 to 85 percent, vegan
- Chocolate chips, semisweet, vegan
- Cinnamon, ground
- Cocoa powder, unsweetened
- Cornstarch
- Cumin, ground
- Dill weed, dried
- Flour, gluten-free, 1-to-1
- Fruit preserves
- Garam masala
- Garlic powder
- Ginger, ground
- Honey

- Italian seasoning
- Ketchup
- Marshmallows
- Mustard, Dijon
- Nonstick cooking spray
- Oats, rolled
- Oil, canola
- Oil, olive
- Onion powder
- Oregano, dried
- Paprika
- Paprika, smoked
- Pasta, gluten-free, quinoa, chickpea, or lentil spaghetti
- Pepper, cayenne, ground
- Pepper, red, flakes
- Peppercorns, black
- Popcorn kernels
- Raisins, golden
- Rice, brown
- Rice, white
- Sage, dried
- Salt, table

- Sriracha

- Sugar, brown, light or dark

- Sugar, granulated

- Sunflower seed butter

- Sunflower seed butter, creamy

- Thyme, ground

- Tortillas, corn, 6-inch

- Vanilla extract

- Vinegar, distilled white

- Vinegar, white-wine

SAMPLE 4-DAY DAIRY REINTRODUCTION PLAN

Now that you have eliminated 1 or more allergens from your diet for two weeks, it is time to reintroduce an allergen to see if you have a reaction. On the next page, you'll find a 4-day reintroduction plan for dairy, which can be used as a model for reintroducing any of the top 9 allergens. You will notice that on day 1 of this reintroduction, you will be reintroducing dairy at each meal and monitoring your symptoms throughout the day and over the following days. You will not include dairy on days 2 through 4 so you can see if day 1 caused any symptoms and whether or not the symptoms went away again when eliminating the food.

	Breakfast	Lunch	Dinner	Snacks and Treats
DAY 1: *Dairy reintroduction day*	Light 'n' Fluffy Pancakes with dairy reintroduction tip *(page 44)*	Kale Chopped Salad with dairy reintroduction tip *(page 63)*	Beef Enchilada Casserole with dairy reintroduction tip *(page 132)*	Peach Sorbet with dairy reintroduction tip *(page 160)*
DAY 2: *no dairy*	Very Berry Smoothie *(page 41)*	Quinoa and Veggie Salad *(page 66)*	Green Chile Chicken *(page 110)*	Hummus *(page 174)*
DAY 3: *no dairy*	Banana Bread *(page 50)*	Mexican Rice Bowl *(page 79)*	Baked Potato Bar *(page 106)*	Guacamole and Salsa *(page 172)*
DAY 4: *no dairy*	Breakfast Taquitos *(page 54)*	30-Minute Pozole *(page 88)*	Broccoli, Chicken, and Rice *(page 122)*	Chocolate Chip Cookies *(page 168)*

MEAL PLANS FOR OTHER ALLERGENS

Because all the recipes in this cookbook are free from the top 9 allergens, you can build each phase of elimination and reintroduction according to which recipes sound good to you! Each time you decide to eliminate a food, you can simply choose any of the recipes in this book for your meals for two weeks. When you are ready for reintroduction, use the tips in each recipe, which are designed to keep reintroduction stress-free.

Now that we have laid the foundation for the elimination diet, it is time to jump into the fun part: the recipes! Get ready for flavor-packed meals and snacks that are easy and inexpensive to prepare. You will never notice they are top 9–free.

Part Two

THE RECIPES

BREAKFAST AND SMOOTHIES

PREP TIME: **5 MINUTES**

I think we have all had moments where we wish we were on a warm beach, toes in the white sand, sipping a delicious cold beverage. This smoothie is sure to satisfy that craving—no plane ticket required.

2 cups frozen peaches

1 (14-ounce) can pineapple chunks in 100 percent juice

1 cup frozen mango chunks

1 cup ice

1 teaspoon ground cinnamon

◆ In a blender, combine the peaches, pineapple chunks and their juices, mango, ice, and cinnamon. Process on high speed or on the smoothie setting for 30 to 60 seconds. Add water as needed and reblend. Serve chilled.

Reintroduce Milk, Soy, or Tree Nuts: Drain and discard the juice from the pineapple. In its place, use 1 cup milk; plain, unsweetened soy milk; or plain, unsweetened nut milk (such as almond milk, cashew milk, hazelnut milk, or macadamia nut milk).

Per Serving (1 cup)

Calories: 88; Total fat: 0g; Carbohydrates: 22g; Fiber: 3g; Protein: 1g

VERY BERRY SMOOTHIE

PREP TIME: **5 MINUTES**

When I think of a smoothie, I think of berries. Put some strawberries in a blender, and I am one happy camper. Berries are packed with nutrients and antioxidants, and they offer the perfect blend of sweet and tart deliciousness to start your day.

2 cups cold water, plus more
  as needed

2 cups frozen strawberries

1 cup frozen raspberries

1 cup frozen blueberries

1 tablespoon freshly squeezed lime
  juice, plus more as needed

- In a blender, combine the water, strawberries, raspberries, blueberries, and lime juice. Process on high speed or on the smoothie setting for 30 to 60 seconds. Add more water or lime juice as needed and reblend. Serve chilled.

Reintroduce Milk, Soy, or Tree Nuts: In place of the water, use 2 cups milk; plain, unsweetened soy milk; or plain, unsweetened nut milk.

Per Serving (1¼ cups)

Calories: 78; Total fat: 1g; Carbohydrates: 19g; Fiber: 6g; Protein: 1g

YOU'D NEVER BELIEVE IT'S A VEGGIE SMOOTHIE

SERVES 4

PREP TIME: **5 MINUTES**

Vegetables in a smoothie? Why, yes! Using super sweet fruit like pineapple completely masks the flavor of the spinach, and carrots have a natural sweetness of their own. Spinach has a very mild flavor, and you can add a handful of spinach to any smoothie and increase your nutrients.

2 cups fresh or canned pineapple chunks (drained if canned)

2 cups packed spinach

1 cup baby carrots

1 cup ice

1 cup orange juice, plus more as needed

◆ In a blender, combine the pineapple, spinach, carrots, ice, and orange juice. Process on high speed or on the smoothie setting for 30 to 60 seconds. Add more orange juice as needed and reblend. Serve chilled.

Reintroduce Milk, Soy, or Tree Nuts: In place of the orange juice, use 1 cup milk; plain, unsweetened soy milk; or plain, unsweetened nut milk.

Per Serving (1½ cups)

Calories: 85; Total fat: 0g; Carbohydrates: 21g; Fiber: 3g; Protein: 2g

SUNFLOWER SEED BUTTER AND BANANA SMOOTHIE

SERVES 4

PREP TIME: **5 MINUTES**

This smoothie is a fun twist on the traditional Mexican drink *horchata*, a sweetened rice milk beverage made with cinnamon. The bananas take the place of white sugar for sweetening the rice milk, and the sunflower seed butter adds a thick creaminess.

4 bananas, sliced and frozen

2 cups plain, unsweetened rice milk, plus more as needed

½ cup sunflower seed butter

1 teaspoon vanilla extract

1 teaspoon ground cinnamon

◆ In a blender, combine the bananas, rice milk, sunflower seed butter, vanilla, and cinnamon. Process on high speed or on the smoothie setting for 30 to 60 seconds. Add more rice milk as needed and reblend. Serve chilled.

Reintroduce Milk, Soy, or Tree Nuts: In place of the rice milk, use 1 cup milk; plain, unsweetened soy milk; or plain, unsweetened nut milk.

Reintroduce Tree Nuts or Peanuts: In place of the sunflower seed butter, use ½ cup tree nut butter or peanut butter.

Per Serving (1 cup)

Calories: 357; Total fat: 20g; Carbohydrates: 39g; Fiber: 6g; Protein: 10g

LIGHT 'N' FLUFFY PANCAKES

PREP TIME: **5 MINUTES**   COOK TIME: **15 MINUTES**

When embarking on an elimination diet, there is no reason to fear missing breakfast favorites like pancakes. You will never believe that these fluffy morning delights are safe for a morning treat.

1 cup gluten-free 1-to-1 flour

2 tablespoons granulated sugar

1 teaspoon baking soda

1 teaspoon ground cinnamon

1 cup plain, unsweetened rice milk

1 tablespoon apple cider vinegar

1 teaspoon vanilla extract

Maple syrup, for serving

1. Preheat a large nonstick pan or griddle over medium heat.
2. In a large bowl, whisk together the flour, sugar, baking soda, and cinnamon.
3. In a medium bowl, whisk together the milk, vinegar, and vanilla.
4. To make the batter, add the wet ingredients to the dry ingredients. Whisk together until there are no lumps. Set aside to rest for at least 5 minutes.
5. Pour ½ cup of the batter per pancake onto the hot pan. Cook for about 3 minutes or until the tops to begin to form tiny bubbles; flip and cook for 2 minutes or until golden brown. Transfer to a plate. Repeat with the remaining batter. Turn off the heat.
6. Serve the pancakes with maple syrup.

Reintroduce Milk, Soy, or Tree Nuts: In place of the rice milk, use 1 cup milk; plain, unsweetened soy milk; or plain, unsweetened nut milk.

Reintroduce Milk, Tree Nuts, or Peanuts: Serve the pancakes with a thin spread of butter, tree nut butter, or peanut butter.

Reintroduce Wheat: In place of the gluten-free flour, use 1 cup all-purpose flour.

Reintroduce Eggs: In place of the baking soda and vinegar, use 1 egg.

Per Serving (2 pancakes)

Calories: 163; Total fat: 2g; Carbohydrates: 32g; Fiber: 3g; Protein: 4g

BLUEBERRY CRUMBLE

PREP TIME: **10 MINUTES**   COOK TIME: **35 TO 40 MINUTES**

Treat yourself to dessert for breakfast. This blueberry crumble is like a fruit-topped oatmeal flipped on its head, with fresh fruit as the base for a delectable crumbly topping.

6 cups fresh blueberries

Juice of 1 lime

2 tablespoons cornstarch

1 cup rolled oats

¼ cup canola oil

¼ cup packed light or dark brown sugar

1 teaspoon ground cinnamon

1. Preheat the oven to 375°F.
2. In a medium bowl, combine the blueberries, lime juice, and cornstarch. Mix well until there are no lumps from the cornstarch.
3. Fill a 9-by-9-inch baking dish with the blueberry mixture.
4. In a second medium bowl, combine the oats, oil, sugar, and cinnamon. Mix until evenly distributed.
5. Cover the blueberries with the oat topping.
6. Transfer the baking dish to the oven and bake for 35 to 40 minutes or until the top has become golden brown and crisp. Remove from the oven. Serve warm.

Reintroduce Milk: In place of the canola oil, use ½ stick butter or serve each square with a dollop of whipped cream.

Reintroduce Tree Nuts: Add ¼ cup tree nuts such as chopped pecans, chopped walnuts, or sliced almonds to the crumble in step 4.

Per Serving (1 square)

Calories: 175; Total fat: 7g; Carbohydrates: 28g; Fiber: 4g; Protein: 2g

STEEL-CUT OATMEAL

PREP TIME: **5 MINUTES**   COOK TIME: **25 MINUTES**

This allergen-free oatmeal makes for a perfect base for experimentation, whether you prefer sweet or savory.

3 cups water   1 cup steel-cut oats
¼ teaspoon table salt (optional)

Sweet Topping Ideas

1 teaspoon ground cinnamon   Drizzle of honey or maple syrup
½ cup sliced fruit

Savory Topping Ideas

1 cup diced avocado, tomatoes,   Dried herbs
   or leftover veggies

1. In a large pot, bring the water and salt (if using) to a boil over high heat.

2. Add the oats and return to a boil.

3. Reduce the heat to low. Simmer the oats for 20 minutes, stirring occasionally. (Keep an eye on the pot because oats have a bad habit of boiling over or foaming up. If this happens, remove the pot from the heat and stir until the oats calm down, then return to the heat.) Remove from the heat. Let sit for 5 minutes to thicken and cool.

4. Serve the oatmeal with the toppings of your choice.

Reintroduce Milk, Soy, or Tree Nuts: In place of the water, use 3 cups milk; plain, unsweetened soy milk; or plain, unsweetened nut milk.

Reintroduce Peanuts or Tree Nuts: Thicken the oatmeal with ¼ cup peanut butter or ¼ cup tree nut butter (such as almond butter or cashew butter).

Reintroduce Eggs: If making savory oatmeal, top with a fried egg.

CINNAMON CRUNCH MUFFINS

PREP TIME: **20 MINUTES**   COOK TIME: **25 MINUTES**

An elimination diet does not mean forgoing baked favorites. Gluten-free and vegan (meaning egg- and dairy-free) baking has been perfected by bakers over the years, and these mouthwatering muffins are no exception.

For the muffins

Nonstick cooking spray, for coating the muffin tin

2 cups gluten-free 1-to-1 flour

1 cup granulated sugar

2 teaspoons baking soda

1 teaspoon ground cinnamon

½ cup plain, unsweetened rice milk

⅓ cup canola oil

2 tablespoons distilled white vinegar

2 teaspoons vanilla extract

For the topping

½ cup rolled oats

¼ cup packed light or dark brown sugar

1½ tablespoons canola oil

½ teaspoon ground cinnamon

To make the muffins

1. Preheat the oven to 375°F. Spray a 12-cup muffin tin with cooking spray or fill with liners.

2. In a large bowl, whisk together the flour, granulated sugar, baking soda, and cinnamon.

3. In a medium bowl, whisk together the rice milk, oil, vinegar, and vanilla.

4. To make the batter, add the wet ingredients to the dry ingredients. Whisk together until there are no lumps. Set aside to rest for at least 5 minutes.

CONTINUED →

To make the topping

5. While the batter is resting, in a small bowl, combine the oats, sugar, oil, and cinnamon. Mix by hand, creating a crumbly texture.

6. Scoop ¼ cup of the batter into each prepared muffin tin cup.

7. Sprinkle each muffin with the crumb topping.

8. Transfer the muffin tin to the oven and bake for 20 to 25 minutes or until a toothpick inserted into a muffin comes out clean. Remove from the oven. Serve warm.

Reintroduce Milk: In place of the rice milk, use ½ cup milk. Or in place of the oil in the muffin batter, use 8 tablespoons unsalted butter, and in place of the oil in the topping, use 3 tablespoons unsalted butter.

Reintroduce Soy: In place of the rice milk, use ½ cup plain, unsweetened soy milk.

Reintroduce Tree Nuts: In place of the rice milk, use ½ cup plain, unsweetened nut milk, or add ¼ cup tree nuts such as chopped pecans, chopped walnuts, or sliced almonds to the topping in step 5.

Reintroduce Eggs: In place of the baking soda and vinegar, use 2 eggs.

Reintroduce Wheat: In place of the gluten-free flour, use 2 cups all-purpose flour.

Per Serving (1 muffin)

Calories: 258; Total fat: 8g; Carbohydrates: 44g; Fiber: 1g; Protein: 1g

ZUCCHINI BREAD

PREP TIME: **15 MINUTES**   COOK TIME: **1 HOUR**

I especially crave this bread during the fall, but because zucchini is available all year long, you can enjoy it anytime you want.

1 medium or large zucchini

1 cup applesauce

¼ cup canola oil

2 teaspoons vanilla extract

1½ cups gluten-free 1-to-1 flour

½ cup packed light or dark brown sugar

2 teaspoons ground cinnamon

1 teaspoon baking soda

½ teaspoon baking powder

1. Preheat the oven to 350°F. Line a standard loaf pan with parchment paper.

2. Grate the zucchini into a large bowl. Add the applesauce, oil, and vanilla to the zucchini. Mix until the zucchini is well coated.

3. In a second large bowl, whisk together the flour, sugar, cinnamon, baking soda, and baking powder.

4. Add the wet ingredients to the dry ingredients. Mix thoroughly until well combined. Pour into the prepared loaf pan.

5. Transfer the loaf pan to the oven and bake for 50 to 60 minutes, keeping an eye on the bread during the last 10 minutes to prevent burning. The bread is done when a toothpick inserted into the center comes out clean. Remove from the oven. Let cool in the pan for 10 minutes before serving.

Reintroduce Wheat: In place of the gluten-free flour, use 1½ cups all-purpose flour.

Reintroduce Milk or Peanuts: Serve a slice of bread with a spread of butter or peanut butter.

Reintroduce Tree Nuts: Serve a slice of bread with a spread of tree nut butter (such as almond butter or cashew butter).

Per Serving (1 slice)

Calories: 156; Total fat: 5g; Carbohydrates: 28g; Fiber: 1g; Protein: 0g

BANANA BREAD

PREP TIME: **15 MINUTES**   COOK TIME: **1 HOUR**

We have a long tradition in my family of buying a bunch of bananas each week, only to watch them go bad. So, we bake a lot of banana bread. This version is moist with a tender crumb, and is perfect for a hearty breakfast.

1¼ cups gluten-free 1-to-1 flour

⅔ cup light or dark brown sugar

1 teaspoon baking soda

1 teaspoon ground cinnamon

3 ripe bananas

½ cup vegetable or canola oil

½ cup plain, unsweetened rice milk

2 teaspoons vanilla extract

1. Preheat the oven to 375°F. Line a standard loaf pan with parchment paper.

2. In a large bowl, whisk together the flour, sugar, baking soda, and cinnamon.

3. In a second large bowl, using a fork or potato masher, mash the bananas until little to no lumps remain.

4. Add the oil, rice milk, and vanilla to the mashed bananas. Mix well.

5. Add the wet ingredients to the dry ingredients. Stir together thoroughly. Pour into the prepared loaf pan.

6. Transfer the loaf pan to the oven and bake for 50 to 60 minutes, keeping an eye on the bread during the last 10 minutes to prevent burning. The bread is done when a toothpick inserted into the center comes out clean. Remove from the oven. Let cool in the pan for 10 minutes before serving.

Reintroduce Wheat: In place of the gluten-free flour, use 1¼ cups all-purpose flour.

Reintroduce Milk: Serve a slice of bread with a spread of butter, or in place of the rice milk, use ½ cup milk.

Reintroduce Soy: In place of the rice milk, use ½ cup soy milk.

Reintroduce Peanuts: Serve a slice of bread with a spread of peanut butter.

Reintroduce Tree Nuts: Serve a slice of bread with a spread of tree nut butter (such as almond butter or cashew butter), or in place of the rice milk, use ½ cup plain, unsweetened tree nut milk.

Per Serving (1 slice)

Calories: 214; Total fat: 9g; Carbohydrates: 32g; Fiber: 1g; Protein: 1g

CRISPY VEGETABLE FRITTERS

SERVES 4

PREP TIME: **10 MINUTES** COOK TIME: **20 MINUTES**

My favorite thing about these fritters is that you can make them with any vegetables. If you have leftover veggies from dinner the night before, crumble them up and add them to the mix.

1 large sweet potato, shredded

1 zucchini, shredded

1 large carrot, shredded

1 cup canned corn, drained

½ cup sliced scallions, green parts only

¼ cup gluten-free 1-to-1 flour

½ teaspoon table salt

¼ cup canola oil

1. In a large colander, combine the sweet potato, zucchini, carrot, corn, and scallions. Put the colander over a large bowl or over the sink and wring out the excess liquid from the vegetables. Discard the liquid.

2. In a small bowl, whisk together the flour and salt.

3. Transfer the vegetables to a large bowl, add the flour mixture, and mix thoroughly until the vegetables are well coated with no flour lumps.

4. In a large pan or skillet, heat the oil over medium heat until shimmering. Line a plate with paper towels.

5. Drop ¼ cup of the batter per fritter into the pan and flatten using a wide spoon or spatula, cooking as many at a time as the pan fits without overcrowding. Fry for 4 to 5 minutes, gently flip, and fry for 4 minutes or until golden brown and firm. Transfer to the prepared plate. Repeat with the remaining batter, making about 16 fritters. Turn off the heat. Serve warm.

Reintroduce Milk: In step 3, add ½ cup shredded Cheddar cheese or serve the fritters with a dollop of sour cream.

Reintroduce Wheat: In place of the gluten-free flour, use ¼ cup all-purpose flour.

Reintroduce Eggs: In step 3, add 1 beaten egg.

Per Serving (4 fritters)

Calories: 242; Total fat: 14g; Carbohydrates: 25g; Fiber: 3g; Protein: 3g

SAVORY POTATO PANCAKES

SERVES 4

PREP TIME: **10 MINUTES**   COOK TIME: **20 MINUTES**

Breakfast is often a sweet occasion, but a savory potato pancake will fill you up and get you ready for a busy day. Zucchini adds a healthy, nutrient-packed twist.

1 pound white potatoes, shredded

1 zucchini, shredded

1 small yellow onion, shredded

¼ cup gluten-free 1-to-1 flour

½ teaspoon baking powder

½ teaspoon table salt

¼ cup canola oil

1. In a large colander, combine the potatoes, zucchini, and onion. Put the colander over a large bowl or over the sink and wring out the excess liquid from the vegetables. Discard the liquid.

2. In a small bowl, whisk together the flour, baking powder, and salt.

3. Transfer the vegetables to a large bowl, add the flour mixture, and mix thoroughly until the vegetables are well coated with no flour lumps.

4. In a large pan or skillet, heat the oil over medium heat until shimmering. Line a plate with paper towels.

5. Drop a ¼ cup of the batter per pancake into the pan and flatten using a wide spoon or spatula, cooking as many at a time as the pan fits without overcrowding. Fry for 4 to 5 minutes, gently flip, and fry for 4 minutes or until golden brown. Transfer to the prepared plate. Repeat with the remaining batter. Turn off the heat. Serve warm.

Reintroduce Milk: In step 3, add ½ cup shredded Cheddar cheese or serve the pancakes with a dollop of sour cream.

Reintroduce Wheat: In place of the gluten-free flour, use ¼ cup all-purpose flour.

Reintroduce Eggs: In step 3, add 1 beaten egg.

Per Serving

Calories: 207; Total fat: 7g; Carbohydrates: 30g; Fiber: 3g; Protein: 3g

BREAKFAST TAQUITOS

PREP TIME: **15 MINUTES**   COOK TIME: **15 TO 20 MINUTES**

Mexican food for breakfast is a family favorite in my house. Eggless huevos rancheros is our go-to, and these breakfast taquitos are an easy grab-and-go variation.

6 (6-inch) corn tortillas

1 (15-ounce) can refried, pinto, or black beans

Nonstick cooking spray, for coating the taquitos

1 ripe avocado, pitted, peeled, and sliced

2 roma tomatoes, sliced

1 jalapeño, sliced (optional)

1. Preheat the oven to 400°F. Line a baking sheet with foil.
2. Place the tortillas between damp paper towels on a microwave-safe plate and microwave for 30 seconds.
3. To make the taquitos, fill each tortilla with 2 tablespoons of refried beans and roll up like a burrito. Transfer to the prepared baking sheet.
4. Spray each taquito with cooking spray.
5. Transfer the baking sheet to the oven and bake for 15 minutes. If you like crispier taquitos, bake for 5 more minutes, watching to prevent burning. Remove from the oven.
6. Serve the taquitos with the avocado, tomatoes, and jalapeño (if using).

Reintroduce Eggs: Scramble 2 eggs over medium heat for 4 minutes and add into the taquitos in step 3.

Reintroduce Milk: Add ¼ cup shredded Cheddar cheese and spread among the 6 taquitos in step 3. Or serve the taquitos with a dollop of sour cream.

Reintroduce Wheat: Substitute 6 (6-inch) flour tortillas for the corn tortillas.

Per Serving

Calories: 537; Total fat: 18g; Carbohydrates: 81g; Fiber: 25g; Protein: 20g

LEFTOVERS TURNED HASH

PREP TIME: **15 MINUTES**   COOK TIME: **15 MINUTES**

Hash is the perfect way to use up leftovers—any vegetables or proteins can be combined for a satisfying meal. You can customize the hash with any of your favorite allergen-free vegetables or proteins.

¼ cup canola oil

1 pound white potatoes or sweet potatoes, shredded

1 bell pepper, any color, chopped

1 small yellow onion, chopped

2 cups packed fresh spinach or kale

Salsa, for serving (optional)

1. In a large pan or skillet, heat the oil over medium-high heat until shimmering.
2. Add the potatoes, bell pepper, and onion. Fry for 10 minutes, stirring frequently, or until the potatoes and onion begin to brown.
3. Add the spinach and cook for 5 minutes or until wilted. Remove from the heat.
4. Serve the hash with salsa (if using).

Reintroduce Eggs: Scramble 2 eggs over medium heat for 4 minutes and add in step 3.

Reintroduce Milk: In step 3, add ¼ cup shredded Cheddar cheese or serve the hash with a dollop of sour cream.

Per Serving

Calories: 222; Total fat: 14g; Carbohydrates: 23g; Fiber: 4g; Protein: 3g

TATER TOT CASSEROLE

PREP TIME: **15 MINUTES**   COOK TIME: **40 MINUTES**

Tater tot casserole is an American dinner classic, but it's delicious as a protein- and veggie-packed breakfast as well. It's perfect for weekend brunch or to make in advance for a quick reheat breakfast.

- 1 pound lean ground beef or pork
- 2 cups green chile sauce (505 Southwestern brand is allergen-free)
- 1 bell pepper, any color, diced
- 1 teaspoon freshly ground black pepper
- 1 teaspoon dried basil
- 1 teaspoon dried sage
- 1 teaspoon onion powder
- ½ teaspoon garlic powder
- 1 pound tater tots (most varieties will be allergen-free; just check the ingredients label)

1. Preheat the oven to 450°F.
2. In a medium pan or skillet, cook the beef for 7 to 10 minutes over medium heat or until browned. Remove from the heat. Transfer to a large baking dish or 9-by-13-inch cake pan.
3. Mix the green chile sauce, bell pepper, black pepper, basil, sage, onion powder, and garlic powder into the ground beef until well incorporated.
4. Cover the mixture with the tater tots, then cover the baking dish with foil.
5. Transfer the baking dish to the oven and bake for 20 minutes. Remove the foil and bake for 10 minutes, or until the top is golden brown. Remove from the oven. Let the casserole cool for 10 minutes before serving.

Reintroduce Milk: In step 3, add ½ cup shredded Cheddar cheese or serve the casserole with a dollop of sour cream.

Reintroduce Eggs: In step 3, add 4 beaten eggs.

Per Serving

Calories: 296; Total fat: 7g; Carbohydrates: 33g; Fiber: 5g; Protein: 29g

FRESH CALIFORNIA BOWL · 64

Chapter Four

SALADS AND BOWLS

HERBED CUCUMBER SALAD

SERVES 4

PREP TIME: **20 MINUTES**

This refreshing herbed cucumber salad is the perfect lunch for a hot, sunny day. It will leave you feeling full and satisfied without weighing you down. This simple base allows for several allergen reintroductions, so you can add it to your meal plan rotation without getting bored.

2 cucumbers, any kind, thinly sliced

1 cup cherry or grape tomatoes, quartered

½ small red onion, sliced

¼ cup distilled white vinegar

¼ cup olive oil

1 tablespoon chopped fresh dill

1 teaspoon table salt

¼ teaspoon freshly ground black pepper

1. In a large bowl, combine the cucumbers, tomatoes, and onion.

2. Add the vinegar, oil, dill, salt, and pepper. Mix the ingredients evenly.

3. Refrigerate the salad for at least 10 minutes before serving.

Reintroduce Milk: In place of the oil and vinegar, use ½ cup sour cream or serve the salad with a sprinkling of Feta cheese.

Reintroduce Eggs: In place of the oil and vinegar, use ½ cup mayonnaise.

Reintroduce Tree Nuts: Serve the salad with a sprinkling of sliced almonds.

Reintroduce Fish: In a medium pan or skillet, heat 1 tablespoon canola oil over medium heat until shimmering. Fry an 8-ounce piece of fish of your choice (such as salmon) for 4 minutes; flip and fry for 3 to 4 minutes, or until the fish is opaque inside and flakes easily with a fork. Serve the salad with 2 ounces of fish per serving.

Reintroduce Shellfish: Serve the salad with 2 to 4 chilled precooked shelled shrimp, such as cocktail shrimp, per serving.

Per Serving

Calories: 160; Total fat: 14g; Carbohydrates: 9g; Fiber: 2g; Protein: 2g

APPLE "PECAN" SALAD

SERVES 4

PREP TIME: **15 MINUTES**

The base of this salad contains no pecans, but it is a perfect way to reintroduce tree nuts as well as other foods. It also tastes delicious topped with leftover chicken.

4 cups packed baby spinach or spring greens

1 Granny Smith apple, halved, cored, and thinly sliced

½ red onion, thinly sliced

¼ cup white-wine vinegar

¼ cup olive oil

2 tablespoons Dijon or honey mustard

1 teaspoon garlic powder

⅛ teaspoon table salt

⅛ teaspoon freshly ground black pepper

1. In a large bowl, combine the spinach, apple, and onion.
2. In a small bowl, whisk together the vinegar, oil, mustard, garlic powder, salt, and pepper.
3. Add the dressing to the large bowl, toss, and serve.

Reintroduce Tree Nuts: Add ½ cup chopped pecans or walnuts before serving.

Reintroduce Milk: Add ½ cup Feta or blue cheese crumbles before serving.

Reintroduce Wheat: Preheat the oven to 375°F. Cube 4 pieces of bread and put on a parchment paper–lined baking sheet. Drizzle with olive oil and sprinkle with salt and pepper. Bake for 20 minutes, making delicious croutons to serve on top of the salad.

Reintroduce Peanuts: Add ½ cup shelled peanuts before serving.

Per Serving

Calories: 166; Total fat: 14g; Carbohydrates: 9g; Fiber: 2g; Protein: 2g

ANTIPASTO SALAD

PREP TIME: **10 MINUTES**

This salad is inspired by classic cheese board flavors. The spicy, earthy arugula is brought to life by briny olives, tangy peperoncini, and slightly sweet red peppers. This dish works equally well for dinner guests or as a quick workday lunch.

4 cups packed arugula

½ cup pitted whole green olives

½ cup pitted whole Kalamata olives

½ cup pitted whole black olives

¼ cup sliced pickled peperoncini

¼ cup roasted red peppers

½ cup olive oil

1 tablespoon Italian seasoning

½ teaspoon table salt

1. In a large bowl, combine the arugula, green olives, Kalamata olives, black olives, peperoncini, and red peppers. Mix thoroughly.

2. In a small bowl, whisk together the oil, Italian seasoning, and salt.

3. Add the dressing to the large bowl, toss, and serve.

Reintroduce Milk: Add ½ cup crumbled Feta cheese before serving.

Reintroduce Tree Nuts: Add ¼ cup pine nuts before serving.

Reintroduce Fish: Toss 1 (5-ounce) can tuna, drained, or 1 (4-ounce) can sardines with the salad in step 1.

Reintroduce Shellfish: Serve with 2 to 4 chilled precooked shelled shrimp, such as cocktail shrimp, per serving.

Per Serving

Calories: 304; Total fat: 32g; Carbohydrates: 5g; Fiber: 2g; Protein: 1g

KALE CHOPPED SALAD

PREP TIME: **15 MINUTES**

I first ate this salad at a restaurant, where it cost way more than any salad should. So I created my own version, and it's now a regular in my lunch rotation.

1 bunch kale, stemmed and chopped

8 ounces tomatoes, diced

1 cucumber, diced

1 ripe avocado, pitted, peeled, and diced

¼ cup olive oil

¼ cup lemon juice

1 tablespoon dried basil

½ teaspoon table salt

¼ teaspoon freshly ground black pepper

1. In a large bowl, combine the kale, tomatoes, cucumber, and avocado.

2. In a small bowl, whisk together the oil, lemon juice, basil, salt, and pepper.

3. Add the dressing to the large bowl, toss until evenly coated, and serve.

Reintroduce Milk: Serve the salad with ¼ cup shredded parmesan or mozzarella cheese.

Reintroduce Eggs: Serve the salad with 2 peeled, crumbled hard-boiled eggs.

Reintroduce Soy: Serve the salad with 1 cup shelled edamame. You can steam them in the microwave for 5 minutes.

Reintroduce Fish or Shellfish: Add a piece of cooked fish (page 60) or serve the salad with 2 to 4 chilled precooked shelled shrimp, such as cocktail shrimp, per serving.

Per Serving

Calories: 247; Total fat: 21g; Carbohydrates: 14g; Fiber: 6g; Protein: 4g

FRESH CALIFORNIA BOWL

SERVES 2

PREP TIME: 15 MINUTES

When I think of California, I think of sun, surf, and amazing food. Fresh fruits and vegetables are the hallmark of Golden State cuisine, and they take center stage in this recipe.

4 cups spring greens or baby romaine lettuce

1 peach, peeled, pitted, and sliced

1 pear, peeled, cored, and sliced

1 ripe avocado, pitted, peeled, and sliced

2 tablespoons olive oil

2 tablespoons freshly squeezed lime juice

1 tablespoon honey

1 teaspoon red pepper flakes

1. In a large bowl, combine the greens, peach, pear, and avocado.
2. In a small bowl, whisk together the oil, lime juice, honey, and red pepper flakes.
3. Add the dressing to the large bowl and mix thoroughly until the salad is evenly coated.

Reintroduce Milk: Serve the salad with ¼ cup crumbled soft cheese, such as Feta, Brie, Gorgonzola, or blue cheese.

Reintroduce Soy: Serve the salad with 1 cup shelled edamame. You can steam them in the microwave for 5 minutes.

Reintroduce Wheat: Serve the salad with freshly baked homemade croutons (page 61).

Reintroduce Tree Nuts: Serve the salad with a sprinkling of sliced almonds.

Per Serving

Calories: 438; Total fat: 29g; Carbohydrates: 47g; Fiber: 14g; Protein: 6g

SOUTHWEST SALAD

SERVES 4

PREP TIME: **10 MINUTES**

If you need a quick meal using what's already in your pantry, this Southwest salad fits the bill. It's loaded with flavor and nutrients, even though it mostly just requires opening a few cans.

1 head iceberg lettuce, chopped

1 (15-ounce) can black beans, drained and rinsed

1 (15-ounce) can pinto beans, drained and rinsed

1 (15-ounce) can corn, drained

1 (15-ounce) can diced tomatoes and green chiles (such as Rotel), drained

1 ripe avocado, pitted, peeled, and diced

2 tablespoons freshly squeezed lime juice

1 teaspoon chili powder

½ teaspoon ground cumin

1. In a large bowl, combine the lettuce, black beans, pinto beans, corn, tomatoes and green chiles, and avocado.

2. In a small bowl, whisk together the lime juice, chili powder, and cumin.

3. Add the dressing to the large bowl and mix thoroughly until the salad is evenly coated. Serve chilled.

Reintroduce Milk: Add ¼ cup shredded Cheddar, Monterey Jack, or pepper Jack cheese in step 1.

Reintroduce Fish or Shellfish: Add a piece of cooked fish (page 60) or serve the salad with 2 to 4 chilled precooked shelled shrimp per serving.

Per Serving

Calories: 381; Total fat: 10g; Carbohydrates: 62g; Fiber: 19g; Protein: 18g

QUINOA AND VEGGIE SALAD

PREP TIME: **5 MINUTES**   COOK TIME: **30 MINUTES**

If you're looking for a grain to fill you up without feeling heavy, quinoa is about to be your new best friend. It's a versatile grain that doubles as a complete protein. Enjoy this salad as is or add more protein to make it even heartier.

1 cup water

½ cup quinoa, rinsed

1 red, orange, or yellow bell pepper, diced

1 cup cherry or grape tomatoes, halved

½ bunch kale, stemmed and chopped

2 tablespoons olive oil

2 tablespoons lemon juice

1 tablespoon honey

¼ teaspoon table salt

1. In a small pot, bring the water to a boil over medium-high heat.
2. Add the quinoa.
3. Reduce the heat to low. Cover and cook for 15 minutes or until the quinoa can be fluffed with a fork. Remove from the heat. Let cool for 10 minutes.
4. In a large bowl, mix together the quinoa, bell pepper, tomatoes, and kale until evenly distributed.
5. In a small bowl, whisk together the oil, lemon juice, honey, and salt.
6. Add the dressing to the large bowl and mix thoroughly until the salad is evenly coated. Serve chilled.

Reintroduce Milk: Add ¼ cup shredded or crumbled cheese of your choice in step 4.

Reintroduce Eggs: Serve the salad with 2 peeled, crumbled hard-boiled eggs.

Reintroduce Wheat: Substitute 8 ounces wheat pasta for the quinoa. In a large pot, bring 4 cups water to a boil. Add the pasta and boil for 10 to 12 minutes or until tender. Drain the pasta and add in step 4.

Reintroduce Soy: Serve the salad with 1 cup shelled edamame. You can steam them in the microwave for 5 minutes.

Reintroduce Peanuts: Sprinkle the salad with ¼ cup crushed peanuts before serving.

Reintroduce Tree Nuts: Sprinkle the salad with ¼ cup sliced almonds or chopped nuts, such as pecans or walnuts.

Reintroduce Fish or Shellfish: Add a piece of cooked fish (page 60) or serve the salad with 2 to 4 chilled precooked shelled shrimp per serving.

Per Serving

Calories: 208; Total fat: 9g; Carbohydrates: 29g; Fiber: 5g; Protein: 7g

BUDDHA BOWL

SERVES 2

PREP TIME: **15 MINUTES**   COOK TIME: **20 MINUTES**

A Buddha bowl is essentially a plant-based dish featuring your favorite vegetables, whole grains like brown rice, and protein from beans or tofu.

1 cup water

½ cup brown rice

½ head cauliflower, cut into florets

1 medium head broccoli, cut into florets

½ head cabbage, any color, cut into 2-inch dice

2 large carrots, sliced

1 (15-ounce) can black beans

2 teaspoons garlic powder

2 teaspoons onion powder

1 teaspoon table salt

1. In a medium pot, bring the water to a boil over high heat.

2. Add the rice.

3. Reduce the heat to low. Cover and cook for 16 to 18 minutes or until all the water has absorbed and rice is tender. Remove from the heat.

4. Meanwhile, bring a large pot of water to a boil over high heat.

5. Add the cauliflower, broccoli, cabbage, and carrots. Boil for 5 to 10 minutes or until the vegetables are tender but firm; you want some crispness to remain. Remove from the heat. Drain thoroughly.

6. In a small bowl, combine the black beans with their juices, garlic powder, onion powder, and salt.

7. Serve each bowl with a bed of rice and a medley of vegetables and seasoned black beans on top, with the bean liquid as a sauce.

Reintroduce Milk: Serve each bowl with 2 tablespoons shredded Cheddar cheese.

Reintroduce Soy: Using a 14-ounce block extra-firm tofu: Line a plate with a thick stack of paper towels, remove the tofu from the package, and place it on the paper towels. Add more paper towels on top of the tofu and put a cutting board on top of the paper towels. Weigh the cutting board down with a heavy book, pot, or several cans. Leave the tofu to be pressed for at least 30 minutes. Cut the tofu into a 1-inch dice. Preheat the oven to 350°F. Arrange the tofu in a single layer on a parchment paper–lined baking sheet. Bake for 20 minutes, flip the tofu, and bake for 20 more minutes. Serve each bowl with ½ cup diced tofu.

Reintroduce Tree Nuts: Serve each bowl with 2 tablespoons cashew pieces.

Reintroduce Sesame: Serve each bowl with 2 teaspoons sesame seeds.

Per Serving

Calories: 508; Total fat: 4g; Carbohydrates: 102g; Fiber: 17g; Protein: 24g

AVOCADO-CHICKEN SALAD

PREP TIME: **20 MINUTES**   COOK TIME: **10 MINUTES**

Although this salad's star is the avocado, any vegetable you have on hand will shine in it. It's an anything-goes salad, and that includes allergens that you are ready to introduce.

For the salad

1 tablespoon canola oil

8 ounces boneless, skinless chicken breast, diced

¼ teaspoon table salt

¼ teaspoon freshly ground black pepper

4 cups chopped greens of your choice, such as lettuce, spring greens, spinach, or cabbage

1 ripe avocado, pitted, peeled, and diced

1 red, orange, or yellow bell pepper, diced

For the dressing

¼ cup olive oil

¼ cup lemon juice

1 tablespoon dried basil

½ teaspoon table salt

¼ teaspoon freshly ground black pepper

To make the salad

1. In a medium pan or skillet, heat the oil over medium-high heat until shimmering.

2. Add the chicken. Season with the salt and pepper. Cook for 5 to 7 minutes, stirring frequently or until the chicken is browned and cooked through. Remove from the heat.

3. While the chicken is cooking, in a large bowl, combine the greens, avocado, and bell pepper.

To make the dressing

4. In a small bowl, whisk together the olive oil, lemon juice, basil, salt, and pepper.

5. Add the chicken and dressing to the large bowl. Toss together until evenly distributed.

Reintroduce Milk: Serve the salad with ¼ cup shredded parmesan or mozzarella cheese.

Reintroduce Eggs: Serve the salad with 2 peeled, crumbled hard-boiled eggs.

Reintroduce Soy: Serve the salad with 1 cup shelled edamame. You can steam them in the microwave for 5 minutes.

Reintroduce Wheat: Serve the salad with freshly baked homemade croutons (page 61).

Reintroduce Fish or Shellfish: Replace the chicken with a piece of cooked fish (page 60) or 2 to 4 precooked shelled shrimp per serving.

Reintroduce Tree Nuts: Serve the salad with ¼ cup chopped pecans, chopped walnuts, or sliced almonds.

Per Serving

Calories: 653; Total fat: 52g; Carbohydrates: 22g; Fiber: 11g; Protein: 31g

CHICKEN COBB SALAD

PREP TIME: **15 MINUTES**   COOK TIME: **10 MINUTES**

A classic chicken Cobb salad includes blue cheese crumbles, bacon, and a cream-based dressing. This allergen-free variation doesn't skimp on flavor but skips the ingredients that are likely to cause indigestion.

1 tablespoon canola oil

8 ounces boneless, skinless chicken breast, diced

¼ teaspoon table salt

¼ teaspoon freshly ground black pepper

4 cups chopped greens of your choice, such as lettuce, spring greens, spinach, or cabbage

1 ripe avocado, pitted, peeled, and diced

½ cup diced tomato

1 tablespoon white-wine vinegar

1 tablespoon olive oil

1 tablespoon Dijon mustard

1. In a medium pan or skillet, heat the oil over medium-high heat until shimmering.

2. Add the chicken. Season with the salt and pepper. Cook for 5 to 7 minutes, stirring frequently or until the chicken is browned and cooked through. Remove from the heat.

3. While the chicken is cooking, in a large bowl, combine the greens, avocado, and tomato.

4. In a small bowl, whisk together the vinegar, olive oil, and mustard.

5. Add the chicken and dressing to the large bowl. Toss together until evenly distributed.

Reintroduce Milk: Serve the salad with ¼ cup shredded mozzarella or blue cheese.

Reintroduce Eggs: Serve the salad with 2 peeled, crumbled hard-boiled eggs.

Reintroduce Soy: Serve the salad with 1 cup shelled edamame. You can steam them in the microwave for 5 minutes.

Reintroduce Wheat: Serve the salad with freshly baked homemade croutons (page 61).

Reintroduce Fish or Shellfish: Replace the chicken with a piece of cooked fish (page 60) or 2 to 4 precooked shelled shrimp per serving.

Reintroduce Tree Nuts: Serve the salad with ¼ cup chopped pecans, chopped walnuts, or sliced almonds.

Per Serving

Calories: 456; Total fat: 31g; Carbohydrates: 17g; Fiber: 11g; Protein: 31g

TACO SALAD

PREP TIME: **15 MINUTES**   COOK TIME: **10 MINUTES**

When you think of a taco salad, you might imagine a deep-fried tortilla shell filled with a tiny bit of lettuce and piled high with meat, cheese, and sour cream. This taco salad is just as delicious, while being much healthier and allergy-friendly.

8 ounces lean ground beef

4 cups chopped greens of your choice, such as lettuce, spring greens, spinach, or cabbage

1 ripe avocado, pitted, peeled, and diced

1 (4¼-ounce) can sliced black olives, drained

½ cup diced tomatoes

1 tablespoon olive oil

1 tablespoon freshly squeezed lime juice

1 teaspoon dried oregano

¼ teaspoon ground cinnamon

1. In a medium pan or skillet over medium heat, cook the beef, stirring frequently, for 7 to 10 minutes or until browned with no pink remaining. Remove from the heat.

2. While the beef is cooking, in a large bowl, combine the greens, avocado, olives, and tomatoes.

3. In a small bowl, whisk together the olive oil, lime juice, oregano, and cinnamon.

4. Add the beef and dressing to the large bowl. Toss together until evenly distributed.

Reintroduce Milk: Serve the salad with ¼ cup shredded Cheddar cheese or a dollop of sour cream.

Reintroduce Wheat: Serve the salad with half of a flour tortilla for scooping.

Reintroduce Fish or Shellfish: In place of the beef, add a piece of cooked fish (page 60) or 2 to 4 precooked shelled shrimp per serving.

Per Serving

Calories: 466; Total fat: 32g; Carbohydrates: 21g; Fiber: 12g; Protein: 30g

KALAMATA CHICKEN BOWL

PREP TIME: **15 MINUTES**   COOK TIME: **10 MINUTES**

Enjoy this Greece-inspired bowl right after preparing it or chilled the next day for lunch, which will heighten the Kalamata olives' flavor.

1 tablespoon canola oil

8 ounces boneless, skinless chicken breast, diced

¼ teaspoon table salt

¼ teaspoon freshly ground black pepper

2 cups baby spinach

1 (15-ounce) can chickpeas, drained and rinsed

½ cup sliced Kalamata olives

½ cup sun-dried tomatoes

2 tablespoons olive oil

1 tablespoon lemon juice

1 teaspoon dried rosemary

1 teaspoon dried oregano

1. In a medium pan or skillet, heat the canola oil over medium-high heat until shimmering.

2. Add the chicken. Season with the salt and pepper. Cook, stirring frequently, for 5 to 7 minutes or until browned and cooked through. Remove from the heat.

3. While the chicken is cooking, in a large bowl, combine the spinach, chickpeas, olives, and sun-dried tomatoes.

4. In a small bowl, whisk together the olive oil, lemon juice, rosemary, and oregano.

5. Add the chicken and dressing to the large bowl. Toss until evenly distributed. Let rest for 10 minutes before serving.

Reintroduce Milk or Wheat: Serve the bowl with ¼ cup Feta cheese or croutons (page 61).

Reintroduce Fish or Shellfish: Replace the chicken with a piece of cooked fish (page 60) or 2 to 4 precooked shelled shrimp per serving.

Per Serving

Calories: 536; Total fat: 29g; Carbohydrates: 37g; Fiber: 11g; Protein: 36g

SPICY RICE BOWL

PREP TIME: **10 MINUTES**   COOK TIME: **30 MINUTES**

From egg rolls to stir-fry, Asian take-out food is a favorite of many diners. This make-at-home version is free of common allergens, endlessly customizable, and just as tasty.

2½ cups water, divided

1 cup brown rice

2 tablespoons canola oil

1 tablespoon minced garlic

1 red bell pepper, thinly sliced

1 cup cremini mushrooms, sliced

1 pound boneless, skinless chicken breasts, diced

2 tablespoons sriracha

1 tablespoon honey

1 teaspoon ground ginger

1. In a large pot, bring 2 cups of water to a boil over high heat.

2. Add the rice.

3. Reduce the heat to low. Cover and cook for 15 to 20 minutes or until all the water has been absorbed. Remove from the heat.

4. While the rice is cooking, in a large pan or skillet, heat the oil and garlic over medium-high heat until the oil is shimmering.

5. Add the bell pepper and mushrooms. Cook for 2 to 3 minutes or until tender.

6. Add the chicken and cook for 5 to 7 minutes or until the chicken is cooked through. Remove from the heat.

7. While the chicken is cooking, in a small bowl, whisk together the remaining ½ cup of water, the sriracha, honey, and ginger.

8. Serve each bowl with the rice, chicken, and vegetables topped with the sauce.

Reintroduce Wheat or Soy: In place of the sriracha, use 2 tablespoons soy sauce.

Reintroduce Soy: Serve the bowls with 1 cup shelled edamame. You can steam them in the microwave for 5 minutes.

Reintroduce Peanuts: Sprinkle the bowls with ¼ cup crushed peanuts before serving.

Reintroduce Tree Nuts: Sprinkle the bowls with ¼ cup sliced almonds or chopped nuts such as pecans or walnuts.

Reintroduce Sesame: Serve the bowls with 2 teaspoons sesame seeds.

Reintroduce Fish or Shellfish: Replace the chicken with a piece of cooked fish (page 60) or 2 to 4 precooked shelled shrimp per serving.

Per Serving

Calories: 392; Total fat: 10g; Carbohydrates: 44g; Fiber: 3g; Protein: 30g

PINEAPPLE BARBECUE BOWL

SERVES 4

PREP TIME: **10 MINUTES**

COOK TIME: **4 TO 8 HOURS**
in the slow cooker, plus 25 minutes

There is something about a sweet-and-savory flavor combo that is so satisfying, and this rice bowl is no exception. Swap in shredded chicken for the pork if you prefer.

1 pound boneless pork roast

1 (14-ounce) can pineapple chunks in 100 percent juice

2½ cups water, divided

¼ cup packed light or dark brown sugar

2 tablespoons ketchup

1 teaspoon garlic powder

1 teaspoon onion powder

½ teaspoon red pepper flakes

1 cup white rice

1. In a slow cooker, combine the pork roast, pineapple chunks with their juices, ½ cup of water, the sugar, ketchup, garlic powder, onion powder, and red pepper flakes. Cover and cook on low for 8 hours or on high for 4 hours.

2. Turn off the slow cooker. In a large pot, bring the remaining 2 cups of water to a boil.

3. Add the rice.

4. Reduce the heat to low. Cover and cook for 15 to 20 minutes or until all the water has been absorbed. Remove from the heat.

5. Using forks or tongs, gently shred the pork; it should fall apart easily.

6. Serve each bowl with the rice, pork, and pineapple chunks topped with the juices from the slow cooker.

Reintroduce Wheat or Soy: Add ¼ cup soy sauce in step 1.

Reintroduce Wheat: Serve the pork on Hawaiian sweet rolls or a hamburger bun instead of rice.

Reintroduce Tree Nuts: Serve each bowl with 2 tablespoons cashew pieces or macadamia nuts.

Per Serving

Calories: 484; Total fat: 10g; Carbohydrates: 70g; Fiber: 3g; Protein: 28g

MEXICAN RICE BOWL

PREP TIME: **10 MINUTES**   COOK TIME: **30 MINUTES**

Burrito bowls are top sellers at Mexican fast-casual chains. This recipe is just as delicious and ready in the comfort of your home in 30 minutes.

2 cups water

1 cup white rice

2 tablespoons canola oil

1 tablespoon minced garlic

1 pound boneless, skinless chicken breasts, diced

1 (15-ounce) can black or pinto beans, drained

½ cup chicken stock

1 teaspoon ground cumin

1 teaspoon chili powder

1 teaspoon dried oregano

½ cup chopped fresh cilantro

Juice of 1 lime

1. In a large pot, bring the water to a boil over high heat. Add the rice.

2. Reduce the heat to low. Cover and cook for 15 to 20 minutes or until all the water has been absorbed. Remove from the heat.

3. While the rice is cooking, in a large pan or skillet, heat the oil and garlic over medium heat until the oil is shimmering.

4. Add the chicken, beans, chicken stock, cumin, chili powder, and oregano. Cook for 10 to 12 minutes or until the chicken has cooked through. Remove from the heat.

5. Serve each bowl with the rice, chicken, and beans topped with a sprinkle of cilantro and a squeeze of lime juice.

Reintroduce Milk: Serve each bowl with 2 tablespoons shredded Monterey Jack or Cheddar cheese.

Reintroduce Wheat: Serve your bowl with a flour tortilla or wrap it as a burrito.

Reintroduce Fish: Replace the chicken with a piece of cooked fish (page 60) or 2 to 4 precooked shelled shrimp per serving.

Per Serving

Calories: 470; Total fat: 10g; Carbohydrates: 58g; Fiber: 7g; Protein: 35g

Chapter Five

SOUPS AND STEWS

TOMATO-BASIL SOUP

SERVES 4

PREP TIME: **10 MINUTES**   COOK TIME: **20 MINUTES**

This simple tomato soup requires little seasoning, allowing the robust flavor of the cherry tomatoes and red bell peppers to shine. The garlic and olive oil add just enough richness to cut through the acid from the vegetables, while cherry tomatoes add a natural sweetness.

4 cups cherry tomatoes

2 red bell peppers, cored and halved

1 tablespoon minced garlic

2 tablespoons olive oil, plus more for drizzling

4 cups vegetable stock

½ cup minced fresh basil leaves

1. Preheat the oven to 400°F. Line a baking sheet with parchment paper.

2. Arrange the tomatoes and bell peppers in a single layer on the prepared baking sheet.

3. Evenly sprinkle with the garlic and drizzle with the olive oil.

4. Transfer the baking sheet to the oven and roast for 20 minutes, turning halfway through to prevent burning. Remove from the oven.

5. In a blender, combine the roasted vegetables, vegetable stock, and basil. Blend on high speed or puree for 30 to 60 seconds.

6. Drizzle each bowl of soup with oil and serve.

Reintroduce Milk, Soy, or Tree Nuts: In step 5, use 3 cups vegetable stock and add 8 ounces milk; plain, unsweetened soy milk; or plain, unsweetened nut milk.

Reintroduce Wheat: Serve the soup with freshly baked homemade croutons (page 61).

Per Serving

Calories: 121; Total fat: 7g; Carbohydrates: 13g; Fiber: 3g; Protein: 2g

BUILD-YOUR-OWN PHO

PREP TIME: **10 MINUTES**   COOK TIME: **40 MINUTES**

Pho is a Vietnamese rice noodle soup that's as soothing as it is delicious. This version, made with easy-to-find ingredients, is quick to put together and can be adjusted to your taste with fresh herbs and hot sauce.

1 teaspoon ground ginger

1 teaspoon table salt

¼ teaspoon ground cinnamon

¼ teaspoon ground nutmeg

4 cups chicken, beef, or vegetable stock

4 cups water

¼ cup sliced shallots or scallions, green parts only

2 teaspoons minced garlic

8 ounces protein of your choice (leftover cooked chicken, raw beef), cut into bite-size pieces

8 ounces vermicelli rice noodles

Optional toppings

Chopped cilantro

Fresh basil

Lime juice

Mung bean sprouts

Sriracha

1. In a stockpot or deep pan, toast the ginger, salt, cinnamon, and nutmeg over medium heat for 1 to 3 minutes or until fragrant.

2. Add the stock, water, shallots, and garlic. Bring to a simmer. Cover and simmer for 30 minutes.

3. Add the protein and cook for 5 minutes or until the precooked chicken is heated up or until the beef is cooked through.

4. Add the noodles and cook for 2 minutes or until tender. Remove from the heat.

5. Serve each bowl with your choice of toppings.

CONTINUED →

Reintroduce Eggs: In a small bowl, whisk together 3 eggs, and once the pho is simmering in step 2, gently pour them in, stirring continually to evenly cook the egg in wispy ribbons.

Reintroduce Wheat or Soy: Add 2 tablespoons soy sauce in step 2.

Reintroduce Soy: In place of the chicken or beef, use cubed firm tofu in step 3.

Reintroduce Peanuts: Serve each bowl topped with 1 tablespoon crushed peanuts.

Reintroduce Sesame: Serve each bowl topped with 2 teaspoons sesame seeds.

Reintroduce Fish or Shellfish: In place of the chicken or beef, add a piece of cooked fish (page 60) or 2 to 4 precooked shelled shrimp per serving.

Per Serving

Calories: 292; Total fat: 1g; Carbohydrates: 51g; Fiber: 1g; Protein: 16g

FANCY RAMEN

PREP TIME: **10 MINUTES**   COOK TIME: **10 MINUTES**

Ramen is beloved just about anywhere, from dorm rooms to the trendiest restaurants. This soul-satisfying version is ready lickety-split.

4 cups chicken, beef, or vegetable stock

4 cups water

2 teaspoons minced garlic

1 teaspoon ground ginger

1 teaspoon table salt

1 brown rice ramen cake (available online)

2 tablespoons canola oil

1 cup shredded precooked chicken

½ cup sliced shiitake mushrooms

¼ cup sliced shallots or scallions, green parts only

1. In a large pot, combine the stock, water, garlic, ginger, and salt. Bring to a boil over high heat.

2. Reduce the heat to medium-high. Add the ramen cake and cook for 3 to 4 minutes or until the noodles separate and are tender. Remove from the heat.

3. In a medium pan or skillet, heat the oil over medium heat until shimmering.

4. Add the chicken, mushrooms, and scallions to the pan. Cook for 5 minutes or until the mushrooms soften. Remove from the heat.

5. Serve each bowl of ramen with a heaping scoop of chicken, mushrooms, and scallions.

Reintroduce Wheat or Soy: Substitute 1 (3-ounce) packet wheat ramen noodles for the rice ones. Add 2 tablespoons soy sauce in step 4.

Reintroduce Eggs or Sesame: Serve each bowl with ½ peeled hard-boiled egg or 2 teaspoons sesame seeds.

Reintroduce Fish or Shellfish: Replace the chicken with a piece of cooked fish (page 60) or 2 to 4 precooked shelled shrimp per serving.

Per Serving

Calories: 246; Total fat: 9g; Carbohydrates: 28g; Fiber: 1g; Protein: 13g

CREAMLESS MUSHROOM SOUP

SERVES 4

PREP TIME: **10 MINUTES**   COOK TIME: **30 MINUTES**

Mushrooms are a wonderful addition to any diet. With a meaty texture that will fill you up without weighing you down, they're rich in vitamins, minerals, and antioxidants as well as fiber and protein. This recipe riffs on the classic cream of mushroom soup but leaves out potentially problematic dairy.

2 tablespoons olive oil

1 tablespoon cornstarch

1 pound cremini or white mushrooms, sliced

1 yellow onion, minced

2 teaspoons minced garlic

¼ cup white-wine vinegar

2 cups vegetable stock

2 cups plain, unsweetened rice milk

1 teaspoon table salt

¼ teaspoon freshly ground black pepper

1. In a large pot, heat the oil over medium heat until shimmering.
2. Sprinkle in the cornstarch and stir until there are no lumps.
3. Add the mushrooms, onion, and garlic. Cook, stirring frequently, for 5 minutes or until fragrant.
4. Add the vinegar and cook for 2 to 3 minutes.
5. Add the vegetable stock, rice milk, salt, and pepper. Cook for 20 minutes or until the flavors meld. Remove from the heat. Serve warm.

Reintroduce Milk, Soy, or Tree Nuts: In place of the rice milk, use 2 cups milk; plain, unsweetened soy milk; or plain, unsweetened nut milk.

Reintroduce Wheat: Serve the soup with freshly baked homemade croutons (page 61).

Per Serving

Calories: 164; Total fat: 9g; Carbohydrates: 14g; Fiber: 2g; Protein: 7g

TOMATILLO-CHICKEN SOUP

SERVES 4

PREP TIME: **15 MINUTES**   COOK TIME: **7 TO 8 HOURS**

A tart cousin of tomatoes, tomatillos are a nightshade commonly used in salsas and in Mexican cuisine. This green twist on tortilla soup provides a tangy punch that's sure to satisfy.

1 pound tomatillos, husked and halved

¼ cup olive oil

2 teaspoons table salt

4 cups chicken stock

4 cups water

1 pound boneless, skinless chicken breasts

2 teaspoons garlic powder

2 tablespoons freshly squeezed lime juice

Corn chips, for serving

1. Preheat the oven to 400°F. Line a baking sheet with parchment paper.
2. Arrange the tomatillos, cut-side up, in a single layer on the prepared baking sheet.
3. Evenly coat the tomatillos with the oil. Season with the salt.
4. Transfer the baking sheet to the oven and bake for 1 hour, flipping halfway through. Remove from the oven.
5. In a slow cooker, combine the tomatillos, chicken stock, water, chicken, garlic powder, and lime juice. Cover and cook on low for 6 to 8 hours or until the chicken has cooked through to an internal temperature of 165°F.
6. Turn off the slow cooker. Transfer the chicken to a cutting board and shred using 2 forks. Return to the soup.
7. Serve the soup with corn chips.

Reintroduce Milk: Serve the soup with 2 tablespoons shredded Cheddar cheese or Cotija cheese or a dollop of sour cream.

Reintroduce Wheat: Serve the soup with a warm tortilla for scooping.

Per Serving

Calories: 310; Total fat: 17g; Carbohydrates: 11g; Fiber: 2g; Protein: 27g

30-MINUTE POZOLE

SERVES 4

PREP TIME: **10 MINUTES**   COOK TIME: **30 MINUTES**

This quick take on a classic Mexican recipe provides a simple but flavorful base to customize to your preferences. Add leftover proteins, like shredded chicken or pork, or vegetable toppings, like cabbage, sliced onions, radishes, or avocado.

2 tablespoons canola oil

1 white onion, diced

2 tablespoons minced garlic

4 cups chicken stock

1 (15-ounce) can white hominy, drained and rinsed

1 (15-ounce) can petite diced tomatoes, drained

2 tablespoons tomato paste

2 tablespoons dried oregano

1 teaspoon table salt

Juice of 1 lime

1. In a large, deep pot or pan, heat the oil over medium heat until shimmering.

2. Add the onion and garlic. Cook for 5 minutes or until softened and fragrant.

3. Add the chicken stock, hominy, tomatoes, tomato paste, oregano, and salt. Cook for 20 minutes or until the flavors meld. Remove from the heat.

4. Serve each bowl topped with a squeeze of lime juice.

Reintroduce Milk: Serve the pozole with 2 tablespoons shredded Cheddar cheese or Cotija cheese or a dollop of sour cream.

Reintroduce Wheat: Serve the pozole with a warm flour tortilla for scooping.

Reintroduce Tree Nuts: Serve each bowl with 1 tablespoon pine nuts.

Reintroduce Shellfish: Replace the chicken with 2 to 4 precooked shelled shrimp per serving.

Per Serving

Calories: 198; Total fat: 8g; Carbohydrates: 29g; Fiber: 6g; Protein: 4g

POTATO, CORN, AND BACON CHOWDER

SERVES 4

PREP TIME: **10 MINUTES**   COOK TIME: **40 MINUTES**

This chowder will make you feel like you've enjoyed a loaded baked potato without the unhealthy cheese and sour cream. With a rich and luscious texture, it's divine to eat and heartier than a broth-based soup.

4 potatoes, peeled and chopped

4 cups chicken stock

1 (15-ounce) can yellow corn, drained

2 bay leaves

4 bacon slices

1 cup plain, unsweetened rice milk

1 tablespoon fresh or dried parsley

1. In a large stockpot or deep pan, combine the potatoes, chicken stock, corn, and bay leaves. Bring to a low boil over medium-high heat. Cook for 30 minutes or until the potatoes are tender.

2. While the soup is cooking, line a plate with paper towels. In a medium pan, cook the bacon over medium-low heat for 10 minutes, flipping halfway through. Remove from the heat. Transfer the bacon to the prepared plate.

3. Using a fork or slotted spoon, remove the bay leaves from the soup and discard.

4. Remove the soup from the heat. Add the rice milk and stir well.

5. In a blender, working in small batches, blend the soup on high speed for 30 to 60 seconds.

6. Serve each bowl of soup garnished with the parsley and crumble 1 piece of bacon on top.

Reintroduce Milk, Soy, or Tree Nuts: In place of the rice milk, use 1 cup milk; plain, unsweetened soy milk; or plain, unsweetened nut milk.

Per Serving

Calories: 315; Total fat: 6g; Carbohydrates: 55g; Fiber: 7g; Protein: 12g

PORK GREEN CHILE

SERVES 4

PREP TIME: **15 MINUTES** COOK TIME: **4 TO 8 HOURS**

Mexican, New Mexican, and Southwest cuisines are staples in my home state of Colorado, and it seems like every family here has its own rendition of pork green chile. This version is delicious on its own but makes for a perfect base for reintroducing wheat and dairy.

¼ **cup canola oil**

2 **pounds boneless pork shoulder,** cut into 1-inch dice

4 **cups chicken stock**

1 **(27-ounce) can whole green** chiles, drained

1 **large white onion, diced**

2 **jalapeños, seeded and diced**

2 **tablespoons minced garlic**

1 **tablespoon chili powder**

1 **tablespoon ground cumin**

1 **tablespoon dried oregano**

1. In a large, deep pan, heat the oil over medium heat until shimmering.

2. Add the pork and cook for 20 minutes or until all sides are browned and no pink remains. Remove from the heat.

3. In a slow cooker, combine the pork, chicken stock, green chiles, onion, jalapeños, garlic, chili powder, cumin, and oregano. Cover and cook on low for 4 to 8 hours (the longer you cook it, the more the pork will break down and become tender and the more the flavors can combine). Turn off the slow cooker. Serve warm.

Reintroduce Milk: Serve each bowl with 2 tablespoons shredded Cheddar cheese or a dollop of sour cream.

Reintroduce Wheat: Serve with a warm flour tortilla for scooping.

Per Serving

Calories: 582; Total fat: 37g; Carbohydrates: 19g; Fiber: 7g; Protein: 43g

ENCHILADA SOUP

PREP TIME: **10 MINUTES**   COOK TIME: **4 HOURS**

This soup combines the hallmark flavors of enchiladas—earthy, spicy, and a hint of sweetness. It's completely free of the top 9 allergens and is so good you'll never miss any of them.

1 pound boneless, skinless
  chicken breasts

4 cups chicken stock

1 (15-ounce) can no-salt-added
  black beans, drained and rinsed

1 (7-ounce) can chipotle peppers
  in adobo sauce

1 tablespoon chili powder

1 tablespoon dried oregano

2 teaspoons chipotle chile powder

2 teaspoons garlic powder

2 teaspoons onion powder

1 teaspoon ground cumin

1 teaspoon table salt

1. In a slow cooker, combine the chicken and chicken stock. Cover and cook on high for 2 hours.

2. Using a slotted spoon or mesh strainer, strain the fat from the broth.

3. Add the black beans, chipotle peppers, chili powder, oregano, chipotle chile powder, garlic powder, onion powder, cumin, and salt. Cover and cook on high for 2 more hours.

4. Turn off the slow cooker. Transfer the chicken to a cutting board and shred using 2 forks. Return to the soup.

5. Serve each bowl of soup with an even mix of broth and chicken.

Reintroduce Milk: Serve each bowl with 2 tablespoons shredded Cheddar cheese or a dollop of sour cream.

Reintroduce Wheat: Serve the soup with a warm tortilla for scooping.

Per Serving

Calories: 263; Total fat: 3g; Carbohydrates: 27g; Fiber: 8g; Protein: 33g

GREEN CURRY SOUP

PREP TIME: **10 MINUTES**   COOK TIME: **20 MINUTES**

Store-bought green curry paste is a great shortcut for packing in a ton of flavor without introducing the top 9 allergens (just check the label to make sure it's gluten-free). It's a perfect, spicy counterpoint to the filling protein provided by chicken in this soup.

2 tablespoons canola oil

1 pound boneless, skinless chicken thighs

1 cup plain, unsweetened rice milk

1 red bell pepper, thinly sliced

3 tablespoons green curry paste

1 teaspoon table salt

1. In a medium pan or skillet, heat the oil over medium-high heat until shimmering.

2. Add the chicken and cook, stirring frequently, for 5 to 7 minutes or until browned and cooked through.

3. Add the rice milk, bell pepper, curry paste, and salt. Cook for 10 minutes. Remove from the heat.

4. Serve the curry as a hearty soup, over rice, or over vegetables.

Reintroduce Milk, Soy, or Tree Nuts: In place of the rice milk, use 1 cup milk; plain, unsweetened soy milk; or plain, unsweetened nut milk.

Reintroduce Peanuts: Serve each bowl with 1 tablespoon crushed peanuts.

Reintroduce Shellfish: Replace the chicken with 16 precooked shelled shrimp, such as cocktail shrimp, in step 2.

Per Serving

Calories: 249; Total fat: 13g; Carbohydrates: 6g; Fiber: 3g; Protein: 25g

SPLIT PEA SOUP

PREP TIME: **10 MINUTES**   COOK TIME: **4 TO 5 HOURS**

Split pea soup is another family favorite. This recipe comes straight from my parents' kitchen. It is so thick and hearty and tastes even better as leftovers.

4 cups vegetable stock

1 pound precooked ham steak, cut into ½-inch dice

1 pound green split peas

2 medium potatoes, diced

3 carrots, chopped

1 small yellow onion, diced

1 cup water

1 teaspoon table salt

1 teaspoon freshly ground black pepper

1. In a slow cooker, combine the vegetable stock, ham, peas, potatoes, carrots, onion, water, salt, and pepper. Cover and cook on high for 4 to 5 hours or until the split peas have begun to break down.

2. Turn off the slow cooker. Let the soup rest for 30 minutes before serving, to thicken.

Reintroduce Milk, Soy, or Tree Nuts: In place of the water, use 1 cup milk; plain, unsweetened soy milk; or plain, unsweetened nut milk.

Reintroduce Wheat: Serve the soup with freshly baked homemade croutons (page 61).

Per Serving

Calories: 657; Total fat: 6g; Carbohydrates: 100g; Fiber: 33g; Protein: 52g

LENTIL AND WILD RICE STEW

SERVES 4

PREP TIME: **10 MINUTES**   COOK TIME: **1 HOUR**

Lentils have been a staple in many cultures' diets since the dawn of humanity. These legumes are rich in fiber, protein, vitamins, and minerals, and they make a complete protein when paired with rice. Rinse the lentils in a strainer to remove any sediment.

8 cups water

5 carrots, coarsely chopped

2 cups dried brown lentils

1 cup wild rice

1 teaspoon dried thyme

1 teaspoon garlic powder

2 bay leaves

2 cups fresh spinach

Juice of 1 lemon

1. In a large stockpot, combine the water, carrots, lentils, wild rice, thyme, garlic powder, and bay leaves. Bring to a boil over high heat.

2. Reduce the heat to a simmer. Cook for 1 hour or until the lentils are tender.

3. During the last few minutes before serving, stir in the spinach, and let wilt. Remove from the heat. Remove and discard the bay leaves.

4. Add the lemon juice and serve.

Reintroduce Milk, Soy, or Tree Nuts: In place of 2 cups water, use 2 cups milk; plain, unsweetened soy milk; or plain, unsweetened nut milk.

Per Serving

Calories: 521; Total fat: 2g; Carbohydrates: 100g; Fiber: 15g; Protein: 31g

CHICKPEA RED CURRY STEW

SERVES 4

PREP TIME: **10 MINUTES**   COOK TIME: **45 MINUTES**

This hearty chickpea stew gets a flavor punch from red curry paste, which is made from chile peppers, garlic, onions, salt, and lime. It can be purchased in the international foods aisle at the grocery store (just check the label to make sure it's gluten-free and does not contain fish sauce or shrimp paste).

2 (15-ounce) cans chickpeas, drained and rinsed

3 cups plain, unsweetened rice milk

1 cup diced butternut squash

1 cup broccoli florets

3 tablespoons red curry paste

1 teaspoon table salt

Juice of 1 lime

1. In a large, deep pot or pan, combine the chickpeas, rice milk, butternut squash, broccoli, red curry paste, salt, and lime juice. Cook over medium-low heat for 45 minutes or until the flavors meld. Remove from the heat.

2. Serve the stew as a hearty soup, over rice, or over chicken.

Reintroduce Milk or Soy: In place of the rice milk, use 3 cups milk or plain, unsweetened soy milk.

Reintroduce Tree Nuts: In place of the rice milk, use 3 cups plain, unsweetened nut milk or serve each bowl with 1 tablespoon cashew pieces.

Reintroduce Shellfish: Replace the chickpeas with 16 precooked shelled shrimp, such as cocktail shrimp, in step 1.

Per Serving

Calories: 274; Total fat: 7g; Carbohydrates: 41g; Fiber: 12g; Protein: 15g

SWEET POTATO AND BLACK BEAN CHILI

SERVES 4

PREP TIME: **15 MINUTES**   COOK TIME: **40 MINUTES**

Chili is most often thought of as beans and ground beef in a tomato-based sauce. This twist, made with chicken and vitamin-rich sweet potatoes, will expand your horizons and is sure to be a staple in your meal rotation.

2 cups water

1 cup quinoa, rinsed

1 tablespoon canola oil

1 pound boneless, skinless chicken breast, diced

20 ounces chicken stock

1 large sweet potato, diced

1 (15-ounce) can black beans, drained and rinsed

2 teaspoons ground cumin

2 teaspoons chili powder

2 teaspoons garlic powder

2 teaspoons onion powder

1. In a medium pot, bring the water to a boil over high heat.
2. Add the quinoa.
3. Reduce the heat to low. Cover and simmer for 20 minutes or until the quinoa can be fluffed with a fork. Remove from the heat.
4. While the quinoa is cooking, in a large pot or deep pan, heat the oil over medium heat until shimmering.
5. Add the chicken and cook for 5 to 7 minutes or until just browned.
6. Add the chicken stock, sweet potato, beans, cumin, chili powder, garlic powder, and onion powder. Bring to a low boil.
7. Reduce the heat to a simmer. Cook for 10 minutes or until the flavors meld. Remove from the heat.
8. Just prior to serving, stir the quinoa into the chicken–black bean soup mixture.

Reintroduce Milk: Serve each bowl with 2 tablespoons shredded cheese.

Per Serving

Calories: 475; Total fat: 9g; Carbohydrates: 59g; Fiber: 12g; Protein: 40g

HEARTY BEEF STEW

PREP TIME: **15 MINUTES**   COOK TIME: **40 MINUTES**

This beef stew is an example of how you may already enjoy elimination diet–friendly dishes and not even know it. It makes for a relaxing weekend meal, with leftovers that are great to enjoy during the workweek.

2 pounds beef stew meat

4 cups beef stock

2 cups water

2 potatoes, peeled and diced

1 sweet potato, peeled and diced

2 carrots, sliced

1 (16-ounce) can green beans, drained

2 celery stalks, diced

1 cup chopped spinach

1 tablespoon tomato paste

1. In a stockpot or deep pan, combine the beef, beef stock, water, potatoes, sweet potatoes, carrots, green beans, celery, spinach, and tomato paste.

2. Bring to a simmer over medium-high heat. Cook for 30 to 40 minutes or until all vegetables are tender.

3. Remove from the heat and serve.

Reintroduce Milk: Serve each bowl with 2 tablespoons shredded Cheddar cheese or a dollop of sour cream.

Reintroduce Wheat: Serve the stew with a slice of soft bread, such as French or Italian loaf.

Per Serving

Calories: 449; Total fat: 10g; Carbohydrates: 38g; Fiber: 7g; Protein: 54g

SOUPS AND STEWS   97

Chapter Six

MAINS

CAULIFLOWER TACOS

SERVES 4

PREP TIME: **10 MINUTES**   COOK TIME: **25 MINUTES**

Cauliflower has a unique meaty texture that is a perfect meat substitute in these fresh tacos. It also has a mild flavor that makes it an ideal base to reintroduce allergens.

1 head cauliflower

2 tablespoons olive oil

1 teaspoon chili powder

1 teaspoon garlic powder

1 teaspoon onion powder

1 teaspoon dried oregano

1 teaspoon paprika

1 teaspoon table salt

Nonstick cooking spray, for coating the tortillas

8 (6-inch) corn tortillas

1 cup chopped red cabbage

½ cup chopped fresh cilantro

Juice of 1 lime

1. Preheat the oven to 450°F. Line a baking sheet with parchment paper.

2. Dice the cauliflower into bite-size pieces, smaller than 1-inch.

3. In a large bowl, combine the cauliflower, oil, chili powder, garlic powder, onion powder, oregano, paprika, and salt. Toss together until the cauliflower is evenly coated in the spices.

4. Spread the cauliflower out in a single layer on the prepared baking sheet.

5. Transfer the baking sheet to the oven and roast, stirring once, for 20 minutes or until the cauliflower begins to brown and is fork-tender. Remove from the oven.

6. While the cauliflower is roasting, heat a large pan or skillet on the stove over high heat.

7. Spray both sides of each tortilla with cooking spray.

8. Working in batches, put the tortillas in the pan in a single layer. Cook for 30 seconds per side. Remove from the heat.

9. Serve each taco with a spoonful of cauliflower, garnished with the cabbage, cilantro, and lime juice.

Reintroduce Milk: Serve each taco with a sprinkle of shredded cheese or Cotija cheese or a dollop of sour cream.

Reintroduce Eggs: Make a simple aïoli for drizzling by mixing ¼ cup mayonnaise, ¼ cup olive oil, 2 tablespoons lime juice, 1 teaspoon cumin, and ½ teaspoon table salt.

Reintroduce Wheat: In place of the corn tortillas, make the tacos with 6-inch flour tortillas.

Reintroduce Tree Nuts: Serve each taco with a sprinkling of sliced almonds or pine nuts.

Reintroduce Fish or Shellfish: In place of cauliflower, add a piece of cooked fish (page 60) or 2 to 4 precooked shelled shrimp per taco.

Per Serving

Calories: 231; Total fat: 9g; Carbohydrates: 36g; Fiber: 7g; Protein: 7g

YELLOW CURRIED POTATOES

PREP TIME: **10 MINUTES**   COOK TIME: **30 MINUTES**

The potatoes in this dish have a creamy mouthfeel from being boiled in curry-spiced liquid. This recipe makes for a perfect, easy, and quick weeknight meal, and the flavor gets even deeper if the dish is enjoyed as leftovers the next day.

2 pounds Yukon Gold
  potatoes, diced

1 (15-ounce) can green
  peas, drained

1 cup plain, unsweetened
  rice milk

1 cup vegetable stock

1 tablespoon curry powder

1 tablespoon ground turmeric

1 teaspoon ground ginger

1 teaspoon garlic powder

1 teaspoon table salt

1. In a large pot, combine the potatoes, peas, rice milk, vegetable stock, curry powder, turmeric, ginger, garlic powder, and salt. Cook over medium-high heat for 20 to 30 minutes or until the potatoes are tender when pierced with a fork. Remove from the heat.

2. Serve the potatoes as a vegan main dish, with chicken, or over rice.

Reintroduce Milk, Soy, or Tree Nuts: In place of the rice milk, use 1 cup milk; plain, unsweetened soy milk; or plain, unsweetened nut milk.

Reintroduce Wheat: Serve the potatoes with warm naan or pita bread.

Reintroduce Peanuts: Serve each bowl with 1 tablespoon crushed peanuts.

Reintroduce Tree Nuts: Serve each bowl with 1 tablespoon cashew pieces.

Reintroduce Shellfish: Serve the potatoes with 2 to 4 precooked shelled shrimp per serving.

Per Serving

Calories: 277; Total fat: 2g; Carbohydrates: 55g; Fiber: 11g; Protein: 11g

FALAFEL

PREP TIME: **10 MINUTES**   COOK TIME: **10 MINUTES**

Falafel is a Middle Eastern staple made from ground legumes, onion, herbs, and spices. This quick and easy take is sure to satisfy.

2 (15-ounce) cans chickpeas, drained and rinsed

½ yellow onion, coarsely chopped

1 cup fresh parsley leaves

¼ cup minced garlic

2 tablespoons cornstarch

1 tablespoon lemon juice

1 teaspoon ground cumin

¼ cup olive oil

1. In a blender or food processor, combine the chickpeas, onion, parsley, garlic, cornstarch, lemon juice, and cumin. Pulse for 30 seconds to 1 minute or until the mixture has a fine texture, but with some chunks remaining.

2. Make each falafel by shaping 2 tablespoons of the mixture into a ball, then flattening into a patty shape about 2 inches in diameter.

3. In a large sauté pan or skillet, heat the oil over medium heat until shimmering.

4. Add the falafel and fry, flipping halfway through, for 8 minutes until golden brown. Remove from the heat.

5. Serve the falafel alone or atop a salad.

Reintroduce Milk: Make a simple dip for the falafel by mixing ½ cup plain yogurt or sour cream with 1 teaspoon minced garlic, 1 tablespoon lemon juice, a pinch table salt and pepper, and a drizzle of olive oil.

Reintroduce Eggs: Make a simple dip for the falafel by mixing ½ cup mayonnaise with 1 teaspoon minced garlic, 1 tablespoon lemon juice, and a pinch table salt and pepper.

Reintroduce Wheat: In place of the cornstarch in step 1, use ¼ cup all-purpose flour or serve the falafel in a warm pita pocket or flour tortilla.

Per Serving

Calories: 321; Total fat: 17g; Carbohydrates: 36g; Fiber: 8g; Protein: 9g

RED BEANS AND RICE

PREP TIME: **10 MINUTES,**
plus overnight to soak

COOK TIME: **8 HOURS**

Red beans and rice are a classic Creole dish. As tradition goes, after a Sunday meal of ham or pork, the bone would be saved for a Monday dinner of red beans and rice. The base for this take on the dish represents the "holy trinity" of Southern cooking: bell pepper, onion, and celery.

For the red beans

1 pound red beans

6 cups water

4 cups vegetable stock

1 green bell pepper, minced

1 small yellow onion, minced

4 celery stalks, minced

3 tablespoons minced garlic

1 teaspoon freshly ground black pepper

1 teaspoon dried sage

1 teaspoon ground thyme

½ teaspoon ground cayenne pepper

3 bay leaves

For the rice

1 cup brown rice

2 cups water

To make the red beans

1. In a large bowl, soak the beans in the water overnight.

2. The next day, drain and rinse the beans.

3. In a slow cooker, combine the beans, vegetable stock, bell pepper, onion, celery, garlic, pepper, sage, thyme, cayenne pepper, and bay leaves. Cover and cook on high for 8 hours.

To make the rice

To make the rice

4. With 1 hour remaining of cooking, in a medium pot, bring the water to a boil over high heat.
5. Add the rice.
6. Reduce the heat to low. Cover and cook for 15 to 18 minutes or until all the water has been absorbed. Remove from the heat.
7. Remove the bay leaves from the beans (though finding a bay leaf in your food is said to bring good luck).
8. Turn off the slow cooker. Serve the beans over a bed of rice.

Reintroduce Milk: Add ¼ cup butter in step 3 or serve each bowl with 2 tablespoons shredded Cheddar cheese.

Reintroduce Wheat: Serve each bowl with a thick slice of French bread.

Per Serving

Calories: 595; Total fat: 3g; Carbohydrates: 115g; Fiber: 21g; Protein: 30g

BAKED POTATO BAR

MAKES 1 POTATO

PREP TIME: **5 MINUTES**   COOK TIME: **1 HOUR**

A baked potato bar is an easy-to-prepare dinner that can be set up to please just about everyone. In a time crunch? Pierce the potato with a fork a few times so steam can escape and microwave on high for 5 minutes.

1 Russet potato per person

For topping options

Leftover shredded chicken, beef, or pork

Steamed broccoli

Crumbled bacon

Olive oil and table salt

Canned chili

Sliced avocado

Minced herbs, including parsley, cilantro, and dill

Sliced scallions or chives

Zucchini cooked in marinara sauce

Barbecue sauce

1. Preheat the oven to 425°F.

2. Scrub each potato under running water to remove any sediment. Pat dry.

3. For crispy-skinned potatoes, do not rub with any oil and do not wrap in foil. For soft-skinned potatoes, wrap them in foil.

4. Put the potatoes in the oven and bake for 45 to 60 minutes or until easily pierced with a fork. (A small potato will cook faster than a large potato.) Remove from the oven.

5. To serve, add the toppings of your choosing.

Reintroduce Milk: Serve each potato with a dollop of sour cream, 2 tablespoons shredded Cheddar cheese, or 1 tablespoon butter.

Reintroduce Soy or Wheat: Serve the potatoes with 2 teaspoons soy sauce (trust me, it is delicious).

Per Serving (1 potato without toppings)

Calories: 292; Total fat: 0g; Carbohydrates: 67g; Fiber: 5g; Protein: 8g

BAKED CHICKEN WINGS

PREP TIME: **5 MINUTES**   COOK TIME: **45 MINUTES**

Chicken wings are an American favorite served at sporting events, backyard barbecues, and bars and restaurants nationwide. Make this crispy classic at home for a fraction of the cost and customize them to your liking.

1 pound chicken wings

2 tablespoons canola oil

½ teaspoon table salt

¼ teaspoon cayenne pepper

¼ teaspoon freshly ground black pepper

2 cups baby carrots

1. Preheat the oven to 400°F. Line a baking sheet with parchment paper.

2. In a large bowl, toss together the wings, oil, salt, cayenne pepper, and black pepper until the wings are coated evenly. Place them in a single layer on the prepared baking sheet.

3. Transfer the baking sheet to the oven and bake for 45 minutes or until the skin is as crispy as you like. Remove from the oven.

4. Serve the wings with the baby carrots.

Reintroduce Milk: Serve the wings with ranch or blue cheese dressing or dip.

Reintroduce Eggs: Serve the wings with a spicy aïoli, combining ¼ cup mayonnaise, 2 tablespoons sriracha, and 1 tablespoon lime juice.

Reintroduce Wheat or Soy: Serve the wings with a soy glaze using 2 tablespoons soy sauce, 2 tablespoons honey, 1 teaspoon ground ginger, and 1 teaspoon minced garlic.

Reintroduce Wheat: Toss the wings in 1 cup panko bread crumbs in step 2 before baking.

Per Serving

Calories: 619; Total fat: 46g; Carbohydrates: 12g; Fiber: 4g; Protein: 37g

CHICKEN FAJITAS

SERVES 4

PREP TIME: **15 MINUTES**   COOK TIME: **20 MINUTES**

Fajitas are a great build-your-own meal that can be customized to any dietary restriction. Here, they're enjoyed with corn tortillas, which are free of top 9 allergens and make a great canvas for reintroduction.

1 pound boneless, skinless chicken thighs, cut into strips

2 bell peppers, any color, sliced

1 large white onion, halved and sliced

1 teaspoon chili powder

1 teaspoon garlic powder

1 teaspoon onion powder

½ teaspoon cayenne pepper

½ teaspoon table salt

8 (6-inch) corn tortillas

1. Preheat the oven to 400°F. Line a baking sheet with foil.

2. Place the chicken, bell peppers, and onion in a single layer on the prepared baking sheet.

3. To make the seasoning blend, in a small bowl, combine the chili powder, garlic powder, onion powder, cayenne pepper, and salt.

4. Sprinkle the entire baking sheet with the seasoning blend.

5. Wrap the tortillas in foil, and place them on the baking sheet without overlapping the vegetables.

6. Transfer the baking sheet to the oven and bake for 20 minutes. Remove from the oven. Serve the fajitas family-style.

Reintroduce Milk: Serve the fajitas with shredded cheese, Cotija cheese or sour cream.

Reintroduce Wheat: In place of the corn tortillas, use 8 (6-inch) flour tortillas.

Reintroduce Fish or Shellfish: Replace the chicken with a piece of cooked fish (page 60) or 2 to 4 precooked shelled shrimp per serving.

Per Serving

Calories: 301; Total fat: 6g; Carbohydrates: 35g; Fiber: 5g; Protein: 27g

MUSTARD CHICKEN WITH PICKLED VEGETABLES

SERVES 4

PREP TIME: **15 MINUTES**   COOK TIME: **20 MINUTES**

This dish combines hearty and filling chicken thighs with the tang of mustard and pickles. You can quick-pickle any vegetable you enjoy.

1 pound boneless, skinless chicken thighs

¼ cup stone-ground mustard

¾ cup rice vinegar

½ cup sliced carrots

½ cup sliced radishes

¼ cup water

½ tablespoon granulated sugar

½ tablespoon table salt

1 teaspoon freshly ground black pepper

1. Preheat the oven to 450°F. Line a baking sheet with foil.

2. Rub the chicken with the mustard. Place it in a single layer on the prepared baking sheet.

3. Transfer the baking sheet to the oven and bake for 20 minutes or until the internal temperature of the chicken reaches 165°F. Remove from the oven.

4. While the chicken is cooking, in a large bowl, combine the vinegar, carrots, radishes, water, sugar, salt, and pepper. Let the vegetables pickle in the liquid for 20 minutes.

5. Serve the chicken with a side of the pickled vegetables.

Reintroduce Milk: Serve the dish with a dollop of plain, unsweetened Greek yogurt.

Reintroduce Eggs: Replace half of the mustard with mayonnaise, and blend the two together before coating the chicken.

Reintroduce Wheat: Coat the chicken in 1 cup panko bread crumbs in step 2 after coating with the mustard.

Reintroduce Soy: In place of either the carrots or radishes, pickle ½ cup shelled edamame in step 4.

Per Serving

Calories: 159; Total fat: 5g; Carbohydrates: 3g; Fiber: 0g; Protein: 23g

GREEN CHILE CHICKEN

PREP TIME: **15 MINUTES**   COOK TIME: **20 MINUTES**

Sheet pan meals are essential to have in your recipe arsenal: They are quick, easy, and require little to no planning or effort. Simply pop the sheet pan in the oven, and set your timer.

1 pound boneless, skinless chicken breasts

2 (4½-ounce) cans diced green chiles, drained

8 ounces canned diced tomatoes, drained

1 small white onion, diced

2 tablespoons minced garlic

2 tablespoons canola oil

1 tablespoon chili powder

1 tablespoon ground cumin

1 tablespoon dried oregano

1. Preheat the oven to 450°F. Line a baking sheet with foil.

2. In a large bowl, stir together the chicken, chiles, tomatoes, onion, garlic, oil, chili powder, cumin, and oregano until the chicken and vegetables are well coated. Spread out in a single layer on the prepared baking sheet.

3. Transfer the baking sheet to the oven and bake for 20 minutes or until the internal temperature of the chicken reaches 165°F. Remove from the oven.

4. Serve the chicken and vegetables alone or with rice.

Reintroduce Milk: Serve each plate with 2 tablespoons shredded Cheddar cheese or a dollop of sour cream.

Reintroduce Wheat: Serve the dish with a warm flour tortilla for scooping.

Per Serving

Calories: 238; Total fat: 10g; Carbohydrates: 10g; Fiber: 4g; Protein: 29g

TERIYAKI CHICKEN

SERVES 4

PREP TIME: **10 MINUTES**   COOK TIME: **20 MINUTES**

The chicken in this dish, another sheet pan favorite, will get caramelized and sticky while roasting, giving it a delightful mouthfeel. Savory, spicy, and sweet—this recipe has it all.

1 pound boneless, skinless chicken breasts, diced

1 cup sugar snap peas

1 cup sliced carrots

2 tablespoons canola oil

2 tablespoons sriracha

1 tablespoon minced garlic

1 tablespoon honey

1 teaspoon ground ginger

1. Preheat the oven to 450°F. Line a baking sheet with foil.

2. In a large bowl, stir together the chicken, peas, carrots, oil, sriracha, garlic, honey, and ginger until the chicken and vegetables are well coated in seasonings. Spread out in a single layer on the prepared baking sheet.

3. Transfer the baking sheet to the oven and roast for 20 minutes or until the internal temperature of the chicken reaches 165°F. Remove from the oven.

4. Serve the chicken and vegetables alone or with rice.

Reintroduce Wheat or Soy: Substitute 2 tablespoons soy sauce for the sriracha.

Reintroduce Soy: Serve the dish with 1 cup shelled edamame. You can steam them in the microwave for 5 minutes.

Reintroduce Peanuts or Tree Nuts: Sprinkle the dish with ¼ cup crushed peanuts or chopped almonds, pecans, or walnuts before serving.

Reintroduce Sesame: Serve the dish with 2 teaspoons sesame seeds.

Per Serving

Calories: 226; Total fat: 9g; Carbohydrates: 10g; Fiber: 1g; Protein: 26g

CHICKEN TIKKA MASALA

SERVES 4

PREP TIME: **15 MINUTES**   COOK TIME: **30 MINUTES**

Chicken tikka masala is a dish of boneless chicken pieces roasted in spices and yogurt and served in a rich tomato sauce. The olive oil in this take gives the creamy, rich mouthfeel that you would normally get from yogurt or heavy cream.

1 pound boneless, skinless chicken breasts, diced

1 (15-ounce) can tomato sauce

1 yellow onion, finely diced

¼ cup plain, unsweetened rice milk

¼ cup olive oil

2 tablespoons minced garlic

2 tablespoons garam masala

2 tablespoons lemon juice

1 teaspoon table salt

1 teaspoon ground cumin

1 teaspoon ground ginger

1. Heat a large, deep pan or skillet over medium heat.
2. In the pan, combine the chicken, tomato sauce, onion, rice milk, oil, garlic, garam masala, lemon juice, salt, cumin, and ginger. Cover and cook, stirring occasionally, for 30 minutes or until the chicken is cooked through and the sauce coats the chicken. Remove from the heat.
3. Serve the chicken alone or over rice.

Reintroduce Milk: In place of the olive oil and rice milk, use ½ cup heavy cream or plain Greek yogurt.

Reintroduce Soy or Tree Nuts: In place of the rice milk, use ¼ cup plain, unsweetened soy milk or almond milk.

Reintroduce Wheat: Serve the chicken with naan or pita bread.

Per Serving

Calories: 297; Total fat: 16g; Carbohydrates: 11g; Fiber: 2g; Protein: 28g

ORANGE CHICKEN

PREP TIME: **15 MINUTES**   COOK TIME: **10 MINUTES**

Orange chicken is a sweet, savory, and spicy delight, which can be made in less time than it would take to get take-out.

½ cup canola oil

1 pound boneless, skinless chicken thighs, diced

½ cup cornstarch

½ cup orange marmalade

¼ cup rice vinegar

¼ cup water

1 teaspoon minced garlic

1 teaspoon ground ginger

Diced scallions, green parts only (optional)

Red pepper flakes (optional)

Cooked rice or steamed vegetables, for serving

1. In a large pan or skillet, heat the oil over medium-high heat until shimmering. While the oil heats, in a large bowl, toss the chicken in the cornstarch until well coated.

2. Carefully drop the chicken into the oil, and fry, stirring every couple of minutes, for 5 to 7 minutes or until browned on all sides and cooked through. Remove from the heat.

3. While the chicken is cooking, in a large microwave-safe bowl, combine the marmalade, vinegar, water, garlic, and ginger. Microwave on high for 2 to 3 minutes or until bubbling, watching carefully to prevent overflowing or burning.

4. Add the chicken to the sauce and toss until all pieces are evenly coated.

5. Serve the chicken with scallions (if using) and red pepper flakes (if using) over rice or steamed vegetables.

Reintroduce Wheat or Soy: In step 3, add 2 tablespoons soy sauce.

Reintroduce Peanuts or Tree Nuts: Serve the chicken with 1 tablespoon crushed peanuts or chopped almonds or cashews.

Reintroduce Sesame: Serve the chicken with 2 teaspoons sesame seeds.

Per Serving

Calories: 333; Total fat: 10g; Carbohydrates: 34g; Fiber: 0g; Protein: 26g

CHICKEN AND TURMERIC RICE

SERVES 4

PREP TIME: **10 MINUTES**   COOK TIME: **20 MINUTES**

With its vibrant color and flavor, turmeric is one of the most versatile spices, and it perfectly complements the satisfying ingredients in this dish. It's also touted as having anti-inflammatory properties.

1 cup chicken stock

2 tablespoons water

1 cup basmati or jasmine rice

4 bay leaves

2 tablespoons olive oil

1 teaspoon minced garlic

8 ounces boneless, skinless chicken breast, diced

2 cups frozen peas

1 cup fresh spinach

½ tablespoon turmeric

Juice of 1 lemon

1. In a medium pot, bring the chicken stock and water to a boil over high heat. Add the rice and bay leaves.

2. Reduce the heat to low. Cover and cook for 15 to 18 minutes or until all the water has been absorbed. Remove from the heat.

3. While the rice is cooking, in a large pan or skillet, heat the oil and garlic over medium heat until the oil is shimmering.

4. Add the chicken and sear for 1 to 2 minutes or until starting to brown.

5. Add the peas and spinach. Cook for 7 to 10 minutes or until the chicken has cooked through. Remove from the heat.

6. Remove and discard the bay leaves. Stir in the turmeric.

7. Serve the chicken on a bed of the rice and top with a squeeze of fresh lemon juice.

Reintroduce Milk: Serve this dish with a dollop of plain, unsweetened Greek yogurt.

Reintroduce Fish or Shellfish: Replace the chicken with a piece of cooked fish (page 60) or 2 to 4 precooked shelled shrimp per serving.

Per Serving

Calories: 339; Total fat: 8g; Carbohydrates: 46g; Fiber: 3g; Protein: 19g

CHICKEN FRIED RICE

SERVES 4

PREP TIME: **5 MINUTES**   COOK TIME: **30 MINUTES**

This take-out favorite can be made at home in a flash. Plus, it can be customized for just about any reintroduction need.

2 cups water

1 cup white rice

2 tablespoons canola oil, divided

1 pound boneless, skinless chicken thighs, diced

1 cup frozen or canned mixed vegetables (drained if canned) or any chopped vegetables you have on hand

1 tablespoon honey

1 tablespoon sriracha

1. In a medium pot, combine the water, rice, and ½ tablespoon of oil. Bring to a boil over high heat.

2. Reduce the heat to low. Cover and cook for 10 to 15 minutes or until all the water has been absorbed. Remove from the heat.

3. In a large pan or skillet, heat the remaining 1½ tablespoons of oil over medium heat until shimmering.

4. Add the chicken and cook for 5 to 7 minutes or until browned.

5. Add the rice, mixed vegetables, honey, and sriracha. Cook, stirring, for 5 minutes or until heated through. Remove from the heat. Serve immediately.

Reintroduce Eggs: In step 5, create a well in the middle of the pan by pushing the rice and vegetables to the edges of the pan. Add 1 tablespoon canola oil to the well and heat until shimmering. Add 2 beaten eggs and slowly stir the eggs until small curds begin to form. Then stir into the rice and vegetables.

Reintroduce Wheat or Soy: Add 1 tablespoon soy sauce.

Reintroduce Peanuts or Tree Nuts: Serve the rice with 1 tablespoon crushed peanuts or chopped almonds or cashews.

Per Serving

Calories: 421; Total fat: 12g; Carbohydrates: 49g; Fiber: 3g; Protein: 27g

TURKEY BURGERS

SERVES 4

PREP TIME: **10 MINUTES**   COOK TIME: **15 MINUTES**

Turkey burgers are a delicious, fresh take on an American classic, and they're lower in fat and calories than beef burgers. The turkey takes on the flavor of the red bell pepper, which also amps up the juiciness of the patties in this recipe.

1 pound lean ground turkey

1 red bell pepper, minced

1 teaspoon garlic powder

1 teaspoon onion powder

½ teaspoon table salt

4 gluten-free hamburger buns or 1 head iceberg lettuce

1 ripe avocado, pitted, peeled, and sliced

1 large tomato, sliced

½ red onion, sliced

1. Preheat the grill on medium-high heat.

2. In a large bowl, combine the turkey, bell pepper, garlic powder, onion powder, and salt until well incorporated. Shape into 4 equal patties.

3. Put the patties on the grill and cook, flipping halfway through, for 10 to 14 minutes or until cooked through and the internal temperature of the patties reaches 165°F. Remove from the heat.

4. Serve the patties on gluten-free buns or in lettuce wraps, topped with the avocado, tomato, and onion.

Reintroduce Milk: Serve each burger with a slice of cheese.

Reintroduce Eggs: Serve each burger with a slather of mayonnaise.

Reintroduce Wheat: In step 2, add ¼ cup panko bread crumbs.

Per Serving

Calories: 313; Total fat: 18g; Carbohydrates: 17g; Fiber: 8g; Protein: 26g

CHICKEN LO MEIN

SERVES 4

PREP TIME: **15 MINUTES**   COOK TIME: **25 MINUTES**

Lo mein is a Chinese dish made with egg noodles, vegetables, and often a meat protein. This variation uses gluten-free pasta and is packed with veggies.

4 cups water

4 ounces quinoa, chickpea, or lentil spaghetti

2 tablespoons olive oil

1 tablespoon minced garlic

1 broccoli crown, chopped

1 orange bell pepper, thinly sliced

2 carrots, thinly sliced

1 pound boneless, skinless chicken breasts, diced

1 cup chicken stock

1 teaspoon ground ginger

Red pepper flakes (optional)

1. In a large pot, bring the water to a boil over high heat.
2. Add the spaghetti and cook for 10 to 12 minutes or until tender. Remove from the heat. Drain.
3. While the spaghetti is cooking, in a large, deep pan or skillet, heat the oil and garlic over medium-high heat until the oil is shimmering.
4. Add the broccoli, bell pepper, and carrots. Sauté for 5 minutes or until tender.
5. Add the chicken and cook for 5 to 7 minutes or until cooked through.
6. Add the spaghetti, chicken stock, and ginger. Simmer for 5 minutes or until the flavors meld. Remove from the heat.
7. Serve the lo mein with a sprinkling of red pepper flakes (if using).

Reintroduce Eggs or Wheat: Replace the spaghetti with 4 ounces egg noodles or wheat pasta.

Reintroduce Peanuts: Serve the lo mein with 1 tablespoon crushed peanuts.

Reintroduce Tree Nuts: Serve the lo mein with 1 tablespoon sliced almonds or cashew pieces.

Per Serving

Calories: 335; Total fat: 10g; Carbohydrates: 34g; Fiber: 5g; Protein: 29g

CHICKEN PARM-LESS PARMESAN

PREP TIME: **10 MINUTES**   COOK TIME: **30 MINUTES**

You'd think a "parm" dish would be off the table in an elimination diet, but as someone who's allergic to dairy and eggs, I had to figure out how to make it work. This version provides a perfect vessel to reintroduce milk, egg, and wheat.

1 pound boneless, skinless
  chicken breasts

1 (15-ounce) can diced
  tomatoes, drained

1 (15-ounce) can tomato sauce

1 tablespoon Italian seasoning

2 teaspoons onion powder

1 teaspoon minced garlic

½ teaspoon red pepper flakes

4 ounces quinoa, chickpea,
  or lentil spaghetti

¼ cup chopped fresh basil leaves

1. Preheat the oven to 425°F.

2. Lay the chicken in the bottom of a medium baking dish.

3. In a medium bowl, combine the diced tomatoes, tomato sauce, Italian seasoning, onion powder, garlic, and red pepper flakes. Pour over the chicken and cover the baking dish with foil.

4. Transfer the baking dish to the oven and bake for 30 minutes or until the chicken has cooked through. Remove from the oven.

5. While the chicken is cooking, bring a large pot of water to a boil over high heat.

6. Add the spaghetti. Cook for 10 to 12 minutes or until tender. Remove from the heat. Drain.

7. Serve the spaghetti topped with the chicken, several spoonfuls of sauce, and the basil.

Reintroduce Milk: Serve the dish with ½ cup freshly shaved parmesan cheese.

Reintroduce Eggs and Wheat: Skip steps 2 through 4 and instead, in a large pan, heat 2 tablespoons olive oil over medium heat until shimmering. Beat 2 eggs and dip the chicken in the egg, then dredge in 1 cup flour. Fry for 3 to 5 minutes per side, then bake in the oven for 20 minutes. While the chicken is cooking, in a medium pot, heat the tomato sauce over medium heat.

Reintroduce Wheat: Replace the spaghetti with 4 ounces wheat pasta.

Per Serving

Calories: 269; Total fat: 2g; Carbohydrates: 33g; Fiber: 5g; Protein: 29g

PEANUT-FREE CHICKEN PAD THAI

SERVES 4

PREP TIME: **5 MINUTES**   COOK TIME: **10 MINUTES**

Pad Thai is a noodle dish that brings together sweet and savory flavors. Using creamy sunflower seed butter in this recipe gives the dish a luscious texture and peanut-like flavor.

6 ounces quinoa, chickpea, or lentil spaghetti

2 tablespoons canola oil

1 pound boneless, skinless chicken breasts, diced

2 tablespoons creamy sunflower seed butter

2 tablespoons distilled white vinegar or rice vinegar

2 tablespoons chopped scallions, green parts only, or chives

Freshly squeezed lime juice, for serving (optional)

1. Bring a large pot of water to a boil over high heat. Add the spaghetti and cook for 8 to 10 minutes or until tender. Drain and set aside.
2. While the spaghetti is cooking, in a large pan or skillet, heat the oil over medium heat until shimmering.
3. Add the chicken and cook for 5 to 7 minutes or until cooked through. Remove from the heat.
4. Meanwhile, in a small bowl, whisk together the sunflower seed butter and vinegar.
5. Add the sauce and chicken to the spaghetti. Stir well to combine.
6. Top with the scallions and lime juice (if using) and serve.

Reintroduce Eggs: In step 3, see page 115 to add 2 eggs.

Reintroduce Wheat: Replace the spaghetti with 6 ounces wheat noodles.

Reintroduce Wheat or Soy: In step 4, add 1 tablespoon soy sauce.

Reintroduce Peanuts: Use 2 tablespoons creamy peanut butter or serve with 1 tablespoon crushed peanuts.

Reintroduce Sesame: Serve the dish topped with 2 teaspoons sesame seeds.

Per Serving

Calories: 380; Total fat: 14g; Carbohydrates: 35g; Fiber: 2g; Protein: 30g

SPAGHETTI WITH TOMATO, SPINACH, AND CHICKEN

SERVES 4

PREP TIME: **10 MINUTES**   COOK TIME: **15 MINUTES**

Although this dish may seem simple, with just noodles, garlic, chicken, tomato, and spinach, it makes for a flavorful, satisfying staple in an elimination diet.

4 ounces quinoa, chickpea, or lentil spaghetti

2 tablespoons canola oil

1 teaspoon minced garlic

1 pound boneless, skinless chicken breasts, diced

2 cups diced tomatoes

2 cups spinach

2 tablespoons olive oil

Juice of 1 lemon

1. Bring a large pot of water to a boil over high heat.
2. Add the spaghetti and cook for 8 to 10 minutes or until tender. Remove from the heat. Drain.
3. While the spaghetti is cooking, in a large pan or skillet, heat the oil and garlic over medium heat until the oil is shimmering.
4. Add the chicken and cook for 5 to 7 minutes or until cooked through.
5. Add the tomatoes and spinach. Cook for 5 minutes or until the spinach has wilted and the tomatoes are tender.
6. Add the spaghetti and stir to combine. Remove from the heat.
7. Drizzle with the olive oil and top with the lemon juice before serving.

Reintroduce Milk: Serve with ¼ cup freshly shaved parmesan cheese or mozzarella cheese.

Reintroduce Eggs or Wheat: Replace the spaghetti with 4 ounces wheat pasta or egg noodles.

Reintroduce Fish or Shellfish: Replace the chicken with a piece of cooked fish (page 60) or 2 to 4 precooked shelled shrimp per serving.

Per Serving

Calories: 361; Total fat: 16g; Carbohydrates: 26g; Fiber: 2g; Protein: 28g

BROCCOLI, CHICKEN, AND RICE

SERVES 4

PREP TIME: **10 MINUTES**   COOK TIME: **30 MINUTES**

You've probably had broccoli, chicken, and rice together before in your life, but this comforting recipe shows that many of the foods you already eat are allergen-free and can be easily adapted to meet your needs.

2 cups water

1 cup white rice

2 tablespoons canola oil

1 pound boneless, skinless chicken thighs, diced

1 large broccoli crown, cut into florets

1 tablespoon chili paste

1 tablespoon honey

1 tablespoon olive oil

1 tablespoon lemon juice

1. In a medium pot, bring the water to a boil over high heat. Add the rice.

2. Reduce the heat to low. Cover and cook for 15 to 18 minutes or until all the water has been absorbed. Remove from the heat.

3. While the rice is cooking, in a large pan or skillet, heat the oil over medium heat until shimmering.

4. Add the chicken and broccoli. Cook for 5 to 7 minutes or until the chicken has browned. Remove from the heat.

5. Add the chicken, broccoli, chili paste, honey, olive oil, and lemon juice to the cooked rice. Cook over medium heat for 5 minutes. Remove from the heat. Serve immediately.

Reintroduce Wheat or Soy: Add 2 tablespoons soy sauce in step 5.

Reintroduce Peanuts or Tree Nuts: Serve the dish with 1 tablespoon crushed peanuts or chopped almonds or cashews.

Reintroduce Fish: Replace the chicken with a piece of cooked fish (page 60) or 2 to 4 precooked shelled shrimp per serving.

Per Serving

Calories: 450; Total fat: 16g; Carbohydrates: 49g; Fiber: 3g; Protein: 28g

KOREAN-STYLE BARBECUE PORK

SERVES 4

PREP TIME: **10 MINUTES,**
plus 1 hour to marinate

COOK TIME: **20 MINUTES**

The sauce in Korean barbecue is sticky, spicy, and sweet, creating a delectable caramelized exterior on the meat. Get ready to be hooked with this quick version, which can be easily customized to your heat preferences.

2 pounds pork tenderloin, diced

1 cup beef stock

¼ cup apple cider vinegar

1 tablespoon sriracha

1 tablespoon maple syrup

2 teaspoons ground ginger

1 teaspoon minced garlic

1 teaspoon onion powder

1 teaspoon table salt

¼ teaspoon freshly ground black pepper

¼ cup canola oil

1. In a gallon-size zip-top bag, combine the pork, beef stock, vinegar, sriracha, maple syrup, ginger, garlic, onion powder, salt, and pepper. Seal the bag and let the pork marinate for 1 hour.

2. In a large pan or skillet, heat the oil over medium heat until shimmering.

3. Carefully drop the pork into the hot oil to avoid splattering and stir-fry for 20 minutes. Remove from the heat.

4. Serve the pork alone, over rice, or with steamed vegetables.

Reintroduce Wheat or Soy: Add ¼ cup soy sauce in step 1.

Reintroduce Tree Nuts: Serve the pork with a sprinkling of sliced almonds.

Reintroduce Peanuts: Serve the pork with a sprinkling of crushed peanuts.

Reintroduce Shellfish: Replace the pork with 2 pounds raw shelled shrimp.

Per Serving

Calories: 332; Total fat: 12g; Carbohydrates: 5g; Fiber: 0g; Protein: 47g

STICKY PORK

PREP TIME: **10 MINUTES**   COOK TIME: **30 MINUTES**

Another riff on a classic take-out dish, this recipe includes instructions for making sticky rice. To save time, however, you can boil rice normally or use boil-in-bag rice.

1 cup white rice

2 cups plus 1 tablespoon water

2 tablespoons beef stock

2 tablespoons honey

1 tablespoon apple cider vinegar

1 teaspoon ground ginger

2 tablespoons canola oil

8 ounces pork tenderloin, cut into 1-inch medallions

1 cup chopped fresh or frozen broccoli

1. In a colander or strainer, rinse the rice several times.

2. In a small pot, combine the water and rice. Cover and bring to a boil over high heat.

3. Reduce the heat to low. Simmer for 15 minutes or until all the water has been absorbed. Remove from the heat. Let sit, covered, for 15 minutes.

4. While the rice is cooking, in a small bowl, whisk together the beef stock, honey, vinegar, and ginger.

5. In a medium pan or skillet, heat the oil over medium heat until shimmering.

6. Add the pork and sear each side for 1 minute.

7. Add the sauce, cover, and cook, stirring occasionally to prevent burning, for 10 minutes.

8. Stir the broccoli into the sauce. Cover and cook, stirring occasionally to prevent burning, for 10 to 15 minutes or until the internal temperature of the pork reaches 145°F and the broccoli is tender. Remove from the heat.

9. Serve the pork and broccoli on a bed of sticky rice with a spoonful of pan sauce.

Reintroduce Wheat: In place of the rice, use wheat noodles.

Reintroduce Wheat or Soy: In step 4, add ¼ cup soy sauce.

Reintroduce Tree Nuts: Serve the pork with a sprinkling of sliced almonds.

Reintroduce Peanuts: Serve the pork with a sprinkling of crushed peanuts.

Reintroduce Sesame: Serve the pork with 2 teaspoons sesame seeds.

Reintroduce Shellfish: Replace the pork with 2 pounds raw shelled shrimp.

Per Serving

Calories: 345; Total fat: 9g; Carbohydrates: 50g; Fiber: 2g; Protein: 16g

SWEET-AND-SOUR PORK

SERVES 4

PREP TIME: **15 MINUTES**   COOK TIME: **15 MINUTES**

Sweet-and-sour pork is my favorite take-out order, and this soy sauce–free version is just as tasty.

½ cup canola oil

1 pound pork tenderloin, diced

½ cup cornstarch

1 carrot, thinly sliced

1 cup canned pineapple chunks, juice strained and reserved

½ white onion, sliced

½ green bell pepper, sliced

¼ cup ketchup

2 tablespoons white-wine vinegar

½ teaspoon table salt

1. In a large pan or skillet, heat the oil over medium-high heat until shimmering. Line a plate with paper towels.

2. While the oil heats, in a large bowl, toss the pork in the cornstarch until well coated.

3. Carefully drop the pork into the oil and fry, stirring every couple of minutes, for 5 to 7 minutes or until all sides have browned. Transfer to the prepared plate.

4. To the same pan, add the carrot, pineapple, onion, and bell pepper. Cook for 5 minutes or until softened. Remove from the heat.

5. While the vegetables are cooking, in a microwave-safe bowl, combine the reserved pineapple juice, the ketchup, vinegar, and salt. Microwave on high for 2 to 3 minutes, watching carefully to prevent overflowing or burning.

6. Serve the fried pork and vegetables with a side of sauce.

Reintroduce Eggs or Wheat: In place of the cornstarch, dip the pork pieces into beaten eggs and then dredge with flour before frying.

Reintroduce Wheat or Soy: Add 2 tablespoons soy sauce in step 5.

Reintroduce Shellfish: Replace the pork with 1 pound raw shelled shrimp.

Per Serving

Calories: 367; Total fat: 10g; Carbohydrates: 44g; Fiber: 2g; Protein: 25g

PORK CARNITAS

PREP TIME: **15 MINUTES**   COOK TIME: **6 TO 8 HOURS**

The herbs, spices, and vegetables used in this carnitas recipe bring out the natural flavor of the pork, which comes out tender and so addictive. You won't need to add anything to enjoy it, but it's definitely ready-made for some classic allergen reintroductions.

2 pounds boneless pork shoulder

2 tablespoons olive oil

1 tablespoon dried oregano

1 teaspoon ground cumin

1 white onion, diced

1 bunch cilantro leaves and stems, chopped

2 tablespoons minced garlic

4 bay leaves

1 cup orange juice

2 tablespoons freshly squeezed lime juice

1. Rub the pork with the oil, oregano, and cumin.

2. Put the pork in a slow cooker. Add the onion, cilantro, garlic, and bay leaves.

3. Pour the orange juice and lime juice into the bottom of the slow cooker, around the pork. Cover and cook on high for 6 to 8 hours.

4. Turn off the slow cooker. Remove and discard the bay leaves. Using 2 forks, shred the pork.

Reintroduce Milk: Serve the carnitas with sliced cheese or Cotija cheese.

Reintroduce Eggs: Serve the carnitas with an aïoli made from ¼ cup mayonnaise, ½ teaspoon ground cumin, ½ teaspoon garlic powder, and 1 tablespoon lime juice.

Reintroduce Wheat: Serve the carnitas on wheat buns or in 6-inch flour tortillas.

Per Serving

Calories: 400; Total fat: 15g; Carbohydrates: 12g; Fiber: 1g; Protein: 52g

PINEAPPLE PORK

PREP TIME: **10 MINUTES**   COOK TIME: **10 MINUTES**

Pork medallions and pineapple rings are a match made in foodie heaven. If you're vegetarian, grilled pineapple is a sweet and smoky treat that you can enjoy on its own.

1 teaspoon table salt

1 teaspoon ground cumin

1 teaspoon ground ginger

½ teaspoon red pepper flakes

1 pound pork tenderloin, cut into 2-inch medallions

1 (20-ounce) can pineapple rings or slices, drained

1. Preheat the grill on medium-high heat.
2. In a small bowl, stir together the salt, cumin, ginger, and red pepper flakes. Rub into the pork.
3. Put the pork on the grill and cook for 10 minutes, flipping halfway through.
4. Just after flipping the pork, add the pineapple to the grill and cook for 2 to 3 minutes per side. Remove from the heat.
5. Serve each medallion topped with a pineapple ring.

Reintroduce Milk: Melt a slice of Havarti or Swiss cheese over the pork medallions before serving.

Reintroduce Wheat: Serve the dish with wheat noodles or on a wheat bun.

Per Serving

Calories: 191; Total fat: 3g; Carbohydrates: 17g; Fiber: 2g; Protein: 25g

PORK SCHNITZEL

SERVES 4

PREP TIME: **10 MINUTES**   COOK TIME: **10 MINUTES**

Pork schnitzel, or *schweineschnitzel* in German, is a thin slice of pork that is breaded, fried, and served with fresh lemon. This version has a mild flavor that pairs especially well with egg and dairy reintroductions.

1 pound boneless pork chops

2 cups gluten-free bread crumbs or rice crumbs

1 teaspoon table salt

½ teaspoon freshly ground black pepper

2 tablespoons olive oil

¼ cup canola oil

Juice of 1 lemon

1. Put the pork chops under a sheet of plastic wrap on a cutting board. Using a meat tenderizer, pound to a ¼- to ½-inch thickness. Remove the sheet.

2. In a medium bowl, combine the bread crumbs, salt, and pepper.

3. Coat the pork chops in the olive oil, then in the seasoned bread crumbs.

4. In a large pan or skillet, heat the canola oil over medium heat until shimmering.

5. Add the pork chops and fry for 3 to 5 minutes per side or until golden brown and cooked through. Remove from the heat.

6. Serve the pork chops with a squeeze of fresh lemon juice.

Reintroduce Milk: In step 2, add ½ cup parmesan cheese to the bread crumbs.

Reintroduce Eggs: In place of the olive oil, dip the pork chops into 2 beaten eggs in step 3 before breading.

Reintroduce Wheat: Use wheat or panko bread crumbs.

Per Serving

Calories: 375; Total fat: 19g; Carbohydrates: 20g; Fiber: 1g; Protein: 29g

STUFFED PORK TENDERLOIN

SERVES 4

PREP TIME: **20 MINUTES**   COOK TIME: **30 MINUTES**

Thin pork rolled around a decadent filling and baked—is your mouth watering yet? When you cut through the tenderloin, a beautiful spiral pattern is revealed, making this dish a showstopper.

2 pounds pork tenderloin

2 cups chopped spinach

½ cup sun-dried tomatoes

2 tablespoons olive oil

2 tablespoons lemon juice

2 teaspoons minced garlic

2 teaspoons dried sage

1 teaspoon table salt

1. Preheat the oven to 400°F. Line a baking sheet with parchment paper.

2. Cut the tenderloin lengthwise down the middle, but not all the way through, like a hot dog bun.

3. Put the pork under a sheet of plastic wrap on a cutting board. Using a meat tenderizer, pound to a ½- to ¾-inch thickness. Remove the sheet.

4. In a medium bowl, combine the spinach, sun-dried tomatoes, oil, lemon juice, garlic, sage, and salt. Spoon onto the pork evenly.

5. Roll the pork into a spiral log and tie with string or secure with toothpicks. Transfer to the prepared baking sheet.

6. Transfer the baking sheet to the oven and bake for 30 minutes or until the internal temperature of the pork reaches 145°F. Remove from the oven. Let rest for 10 minutes before slicing and serving.

Reintroduce Milk: In step 4, add ½ cup cream cheese or shredded mozzarella cheese.

Reintroduce Eggs: Brush 2 beaten eggs on the exterior of the pork tenderloin as an egg wash in step 5.

Reintroduce Wheat: In step 4, add ½ cup panko bread crumbs.

Reintroduce Tree Nuts: In step 4, add ½ cup crushed pine nuts.

Per Serving

Calories: 333; Total fat: 12g; Carbohydrates: 6g; Fiber: 1g; Protein: 49g

ONE-PAN MEATBALLS

SERVES 4

PREP TIME: **10 MINUTES**   COOK TIME: **30 MINUTES**

Meatballs are traditionally made with at least one top 9 allergen, and many recipes call for a few of them! This elimination diet–friendly version is simple to make, and with some gentle handling, these meatballs hold together just as well as their traditional counterparts.

1 pound lean ground beef

1 bunch parsley leaves and stems, minced

2 tablespoons olive oil

1 (15-ounce) can tomato sauce

1 tablespoon Italian seasoning

1 teaspoon garlic powder

1 teaspoon onion powder

¼ cup beef stock

1. In a large bowl, mix together the beef and parsley. Roll tightly into small meatballs, about 2 tablespoons in size. The mixture should make 20 meatballs.

2. In a large pan or skillet, heat the oil over medium heat until shimmering.

3. Add the meatballs and cook for 10 minutes, turning until all sides are browned.

4. Add the tomato sauce, Italian seasoning, garlic powder, and onion powder. Bring to a low boil.

5. Add the beef stock. Using a wooden spoon, gently scrape the bottom of the pan to deglaze. Cover and cook for 10 minutes. Remove from the heat. Serve immediately.

Reintroduce Milk: Melt ¼ cup mozzarella cheese over the meatballs in step 5 before serving.

Reintroduce Eggs: In step 1, add 2 beaten eggs.

Reintroduce Wheat: In step 1, use ¼ cup wheat or panko bread crumbs or serve the meatballs over wheat pasta or in a hoagie roll for a meatball sub.

Per Serving

Calories: 244; Total fat: 13g; Carbohydrates: 8g; Fiber: 2g; Protein: 26g

BEEF ENCHILADA CASSEROLE

PREP TIME: **10 MINUTES**   COOK TIME: **40 MINUTES**

This recipe is a fun mash-up between enchiladas and lasagna, layering tortillas, beef, veggies, and sauce to create a one-pan casserole-style bake.

1 pound lean ground beef

2 zucchini, shredded

1 (15-ounce) can fire-roasted tomatoes, drained

1 teaspoon garlic powder

½ teaspoon ground cinnamon

½ teaspoon table salt

¼ teaspoon ground cumin

12 (6-inch) corn tortillas

1 tablespoon olive oil

1. Preheat the oven to 350°F.

2. Heat a large nonstick pan or skillet over medium heat. Cook the beef in the pan for 5 to 7 minutes or until browned. Remove from the heat.

3. To make the filling, in a large bowl, combine the beef, zucchini, tomatoes, garlic powder, cinnamon, salt, and cumin. Mix well.

4. Cover the bottom of a 9-inch square baking dish with 4 corn tortillas.

5. Add half of the filling, pushing it to all the edges of the dish. Cover with 4 more tortillas.

6. Add the remaining half of the filling and cover with the last 4 tortillas.

7. Brush the top layer with the oil and cover with foil.

8. Transfer the baking dish to the oven and bake for 20 minutes. Remove the foil and bake for 10 minutes or until the top is golden and bubbly. Remove from the oven. Serve by the spoonful.

Reintroduce Milk: In step 5, add ½ cup shredded Cheddar or Monterey Jack cheese to the top layer.

Reintroduce Wheat: Use flour tortillas in place of the corn tortillas.

Per Serving

Calories: 389; Total fat: 12g; Carbohydrates: 44g; Fiber: 7g; Protein: 31g

NOT-YOUR-TRADITIONAL MONGOLIAN BEEF

SERVES 4

PREP TIME: **15 MINUTES**   COOK TIME: **15 MINUTES**

Despite the name, Mongolian beef is actually a Taiwanese dish that's gained popularity around the world. It's a great way to test out soy, wheat, sesame, and even nuts if you're so inclined.

¾ cup beef stock

½ cup light or dark brown sugar

3 tablespoons canola oil

2 teaspoons ground ginger

2 teaspoons minced garlic

¼ teaspoon red pepper flakes

1 pound flank steak, cut into 1-inch strips

2 cups broccoli florets or fresh green beans

¼ cup sliced scallions, green parts only

1. In a large, deep pan or skillet, combine the beef stock, sugar, oil, ginger, garlic, and red pepper flakes. Cook over medium-high heat for 5 minutes or until the mixture reaches a low boil.

2. Add the steak and broccoli. Cook for 10 minutes or until the steak has cooked through and the broccoli is tender. Remove from the heat.

3. Serve the beef garnished with the scallions, alone, or over rice.

Reintroduce Wheat: Serve the dish over wheat noodles.

Reintroduce Wheat or Soy: Add 2 tablespoons soy sauce in step 1.

Reintroduce Soy: In place of the broccoli or green beans, use 2 cups edamame.

Reintroduce Tree Nuts: Serve the dish with 2 tablespoons sliced almonds.

Reintroduce Peanuts: Serve the dish with 2 tablespoons crushed peanuts.

Reintroduce Sesame: Serve the dish with 2 teaspoons sesame seeds.

Per Serving

Calories: 374; Total fat: 16g; Carbohydrates: 31g; Fiber: 1g; Protein: 26g

MINI MEATLOAVES

SERVES 4

PREP TIME: **15 MINUTES**   COOK TIME: **1 HOUR 10 MINUTES**

Enjoy this recipe as a fresh take on your mother's meatloaf. A slice paired with some steamed vegetables makes the perfect meal.

1 cup water

½ cup white rice

1 pound lean ground beef

8 ounces button mushrooms, minced

1 green bell pepper, finely chopped

1 bunch parsley, minced

1 tablespoon minced garlic

3 tablespoons ketchup

1. Preheat the oven to 350°F. Line a 6-cup large-well muffin tin or a mini loaf pan with parchment paper.

2. In a medium pot, bring the water to a boil over high heat. Add the rice.

3. Reduce the heat to low. Cover and cook for 15 to 18 minutes or until all the water has been absorbed. Remove from the heat.

4. In a large bowl, combine the beef, mushrooms, bell pepper, parsley, garlic, ketchup, and rice. Using clean or gloved hands, mash together until all the ingredients are evenly distributed. Pack into the wells.

5. Transfer the muffin tin to the oven and bake for 35 to 45 minutes or until no pink remains in the center of the meatloaves. (Baking longer will just give a more caramelized crust.) Remove from the oven. Let rest for 10 minutes before serving.

Reintroduce Milk: Add ½ cup shredded Cheddar cheese in step 4 to make cheeseburger meatloaf.

Reintroduce Eggs: Add 2 beaten eggs in step 4.

Reintroduce Wheat: In place of the rice, use 1 cup bread crumbs and ½ cup beef stock.

Reintroduce Wheat or Soy: Add 2 tablespoons Worcestershire sauce in step 4.

Per Serving

Calories: 278; Total fat: 6g; Carbohydrates: 28g; Fiber: 2g; Protein: 29g

GARLIC BUTTER-LESS STEAK TIPS

SERVES 4

These steak tips are so quick and easy, you can use them as the base for any meal—breakfast, lunch, or dinner. Garlic butter may be delicious, but garlic olive oil is just as tasty!

¼ cup olive oil

1 tablespoon minced garlic

1½ pounds steak of your choice (rib eye, sirloin, New York strip), diced

2 teaspoons light or dark brown sugar

2 teaspoons chili powder

1 teaspoon table salt

¼ teaspoon cayenne pepper

¼ cup sliced scallions, green parts only

1. In a large pan or skillet, heat the oil and garlic over medium-high heat until the oil is shimmering. Line a plate with paper towels.

2. While the oil and garlic are heating, in a large bowl, toss together the steak, sugar, chili powder, salt, and cayenne pepper until the steak is evenly coated.

3. Reduce the heat to medium. Add the steak and fry for 2 to 3 minutes per side or until browned. Remove from the heat. The steak may be slightly pink in the middle. Transfer to the prepared plate.

4. Serve the steak topped with the scallions.

Reintroduce Milk: In place of the olive oil, use ¼ cup butter.

Reintroduce Eggs: Serve the steak with scrambled eggs for a delicious breakfast-for-dinner.

Reintroduce Wheat: Serve the steak with wheat noodles.

Per Serving

Calories: 441; Total fat: 31g; Carbohydrates: 4g; Fiber: 1g; Protein: 34g

BEEF STROGANOFF

PREP TIME: **10 MINUTES**   COOK TIME: **30 MINUTES**

Traditional beef stroganoff is a Russian dish featuring beef in sour cream sauce. Enjoy it on the elimination diet with a few simple modifications.

1 cup water

½ cup rice

1 pound lean ground beef

8 ounces button mushrooms, sliced

2 cups plain, unsweetened rice milk

2 tablespoons Dijon mustard

¼ cup beef stock

2 tablespoons cornstarch

2 tablespoons minced fresh parsley

1. In a medium pot, bring the water to a boil over high heat. Add the rice.

2. Reduce the heat to low. Cover and cook for 15 to 18 minutes or until all the water has been absorbed. Remove from the heat.

3. While the rice is cooking, in a large pan or skillet, cook the beef for 7 to 10 minutes over medium heat or until browned.

4. Increase the heat to medium-high. Add the mushrooms, rice milk, and mustard. Cook for 10 minutes or until the flavors meld.

5. In a small bowl, whisk together the beef stock and cornstarch. Stir into the pan and cook for 5 minutes. Remove from the heat. Let cool and thicken for 10 minutes.

6. Serve the stroganoff topped with the parsley.

Reintroduce Milk: In place of the rice milk, use 2 cups milk, or serve the stroganoff with a dollop of sour cream.

Reintroduce Eggs or Wheat: In place of the rice, serve the stroganoff over 8 ounces egg noodles.

Reintroduce Wheat or Soy: Add 2 teaspoons Worcestershire sauce in step 5.

Reintroduce Soy or Tree Nuts: In place of the rice milk, use 2 cups plain, unsweetened soy milk or plain, unsweetened almond milk.

Per Serving

Calories: 319; Total fat: 8g; Carbohydrates: 29g; Fiber: 2g; Protein: 32g

STEAK, PEPPERS, AND ONIONS

SERVES 4

PREP TIME: **15 MINUTES**   COOK TIME: **15 MINUTES**

Steak, peppers, and onions go perfectly together in fajitas, Philly cheesesteaks, and fine-dining dishes. The best part is that when you make it at home, it's ready in less than a half hour.

2 tablespoons olive oil

1 large white onion, sliced

1 red bell pepper, sliced

1 yellow bell pepper, sliced

1 pound flank steak, cut into strips

1 teaspoon dried basil

½ teaspoon table salt

½ teaspoon freshly ground black pepper

1. In a large pan or skillet, heat the oil over medium heat until shimmering.

2. Add the onion, red bell pepper, and yellow bell pepper. Cook for 5 minutes or until browned.

3. While the vegetables are cooking, season the steak with the basil, salt, and pepper.

4. Add the steak to the pan and cook for 5 more minutes or until cooked through. Remove from the heat.

Reintroduce Wheat: Serve the dish with wheat noodles, on a hoagie roll, or in flour tortillas.

Reintroduce Wheat or Soy: Add 1 tablespoon soy sauce in step 3.

Reintroduce Milk: Serve the dish with ¼ cup melted pepper Jack or Monterey Jack cheese.

Reintroduce Shellfish: In place of the steak, use 1 pound raw, peeled shrimp.

Per Serving

Calories: 284; Total fat: 16g; Carbohydrates: 8g; Fiber: 2g; Protein: 25g

SHEPHERD'S PIE

PREP TIME: **10 MINUTES**   COOK TIME: **35 MINUTES**

What we commonly refer to as shepherd's pie is an English dish called cottage pie. True shepherd's pie is an Irish classic that contains lamb, whereas the English version contains beef. This is a great recipe to prep ahead of time and freeze for a quick bake when you need a pre-prepared meal. Store leftovers in freezer-safe containers and reheat in an oven-safe dish for 1 hour at 400°F.

2 pounds white potatoes, diced

1 pound lean ground beef

¼ cup beef stock

2 tablespoons olive oil

15 ounces green peas, fresh, frozen, or canned (drained if canned)

1 (8-ounce) can tomato sauce

1 teaspoon dried rosemary

1. Preheat the oven to 400°F. Bring a large pot of water to a boil over high heat.

2. Add the potatoes and cook for 15 minutes or until tender when pierced with a fork. Strain the potatoes, reserving a few tablespoons of the starchy liquid for mashing. Return the potatoes and reserved liquid to the pot.

3. While the potatoes are boiling, in a medium pan or skillet, cook the beef over medium heat for 7 to 10 minutes or until browned. Remove from the heat.

4. Add the beef stock and oil to the cooked potatoes. Mash the potatoes until there are no lumps.

5. In a 9-inch square baking dish, stir together the beef, peas, tomato sauce, and rosemary until well incorporated.

6. Spread the mashed potatoes over the beef mixture.

7. Transfer the baking dish to the oven. Bake for 20 minutes or until the top is golden and bubbly. Remove from the oven. Let rest for 10 minutes before serving.

138   THE ELIMINATION DIET COOKBOOK

Reintroduce Milk: In place of the olive oil, use 2 tablespoons butter in step 4; in place of the beef stock, use ¼ cup milk in step 4 or spread ¼ cup shredded Cheddar cheese over the top in step 6.

Reintroduce Wheat or Soy: Add 1 teaspoon Worcestershire sauce in step 4.

Per Serving

Calories: 522; Total fat: 13g; Carbohydrates: 66g; Fiber: 11g; Protein: 36g

Chapter Seven

VEGETABLES AND SIDES

ZUCCHINI CHIPS

PREP TIME: **15 MINUTES**   COOK TIME: **2 HOURS**

These zucchini chips are a healthy alternative to potato chips. Season them however you like since they take on any flavor beautifully.

3 pounds zucchini

3 tablespoons olive oil

½ teaspoon table salt

¼ teaspoon freshly ground black pepper

1. Preheat the oven to 225°F. Line a baking sheet with parchment paper.
2. Using a mandoline or a very sharp knife, shave the zucchini into very thin slices.
3. Lay as many zucchini slices as you can in a single layer on the prepared baking sheet.
4. Drizzle the zucchini with the oil. Season with the salt and pepper.
5. Transfer the baking sheet to the oven and bake for 2 hours or until the zucchini are golden brown and crispy like chips. Remove from the oven. Let cool before serving.

Reintroduce Milk: Serve the chips with a sour cream or yogurt dip.

Reintroduce Eggs: Serve the chips with spicy aïoli (page 107).

Reintroduce Soy: Serve the chips with a yogurt dip made from soy yogurt.

Reintroduce Fish or Shellfish: Serve the chips with a piece of fish (page 60) or shellfish as the main course.

Per Serving

Calories: 162; Total fat: 11g; Carbohydrates: 11g; Fiber: 4g; Protein: 9g

ZUCCHINI FRIES

SERVES 4

PREP TIME: **15 MINUTES**   COOK TIME: **30 MINUTES**

These are not so much an alternative to French fries but rather a completely different side dish. They're a crispy and tender, dippable finger food.

2 pounds zucchini

2 tablespoons olive oil

½ teaspoon table salt

½ teaspoon paprika

1. Preheat the oven to 425°F. Line a baking sheet with parchment paper.
2. Cut the zucchini into strips measuring ½ inch by a few inches.
3. Place the zucchini in a single layer on the prepared baking sheet.
4. Drizzle the zucchini with the oil. Season with the salt and paprika.
5. Transfer the baking sheet to the oven and bake, flipping halfway through, for 30 minutes or until the fries are golden brown. Remove from the oven.

Reintroduce Milk: Serve the fries with a sour cream or yogurt dip or coat in ¼ cup parmesan cheese.

Reintroduce Eggs: Serve the fries with spicy aïoli (page 107).

Reintroduce Soy: Serve the fries with a yogurt dip made from soy yogurt.

Reintroduce Wheat: Coat the zucchini in panko bread crumbs before baking.

Reintroduce Fish or Shellfish: Serve the fries with a piece of fish (page 60) or shellfish as the main course.

Per Serving

Calories: 108; Total fat: 8g; Carbohydrates: 7g; Fiber: 3g; Protein: 6g

COLESLAW

SERVES 4

PREP TIME: **10 MINUTES**

Coleslaw is a crisp and cool side dish enjoyed at barbecues all summer long. Many coleslaws are mayonnaise based, but it is super simple to make top 9-free coleslaw and modify to your needs.

1 head cabbage, or ½ head red cabbage and ½ head green cabbage, shredded

2 cups shredded carrots

½ cup Dijon mustard

2 tablespoons apple cider vinegar

½ teaspoon sugar

½ teaspoon table salt

½ teaspoon freshly ground black pepper

◆ In a large bowl, toss together the cabbage, carrots, mustard, vinegar, sugar, salt, and pepper. Refrigerate for at least 10 minutes before serving.

Reintroduce Eggs: In place of the vinegar and mustard, use ½ cup mayonnaise.

Reintroduce Tree Nuts: Serve the coleslaw with 2 tablespoons sliced almonds.

Reintroduce Fish or Shellfish: Serve the coleslaw with a piece of fish (page 60) or shellfish as the main course.

Per Serving

Calories: 89; Total fat: 1g; Carbohydrates: 18g; Fiber: 6g; Protein: 4g

RICED CAULIFLOWER WITH MUSHROOMS AND SPINACH

PREP TIME: **15 MINUTES**   COOK TIME: **10 MINUTES**

Cauliflower rice is the perfect substitute for grains in any dish. It has a wonderful texture and a mild flavor that pairs especially well with the mushroom, spinach, and vibrant seasoning in this recipe.

1 head cauliflower, leaves removed

2 tablespoons olive oil

1 teaspoon minced garlic

2 cups packed fresh spinach

1 cup diced mushrooms

½ teaspoon table salt

½ teaspoon red pepper flakes

1. Using the large holes on a box grater, grate the cauliflower to create "rice."

2. In a large pan or skillet, heat the oil and garlic over medium heat until the oil is shimmering.

3. Add the cauliflower rice, spinach, mushrooms, salt, and red pepper flakes. Cook for 10 minutes or until tender. Remove from the heat. Serve warm.

Reintroduce Milk: Add ¼ cup parmesan cheese in step 3.

Reintroduce Tree Nuts: Add 2 tablespoons sliced almonds in step 3.

Reintroduce Fish or Shellfish: Serve the dish with a piece of fish (page 60) or shellfish as the main course.

Per Serving

Calories: 105; Total fat: 7g; Carbohydrates: 9g; Fiber: 4g; Protein: 4g

GLAZED CARROTS

PREP TIME: **10 MINUTES**   COOK TIME: **15 MINUTES**

Simple ingredients and cooking methods are what define a perfect side dish to me. These glazed carrots are an ideal companion to any meal and sophisticated enough to serve at a holiday meal.

1 pound whole carrots, cut on a
  bias into ½-inch-thick slices

1 cup water

1 tablespoon maple syrup

1 tablespoon olive oil

1 teaspoon ground ginger

¼ teaspoon table salt

½ teaspoon freshly ground
  black pepper

1. In a large pan or skillet, combine the carrots and water. Bring to a simmer over medium-high heat. Cook for 10 minutes or until tender. Drain and return the carrots to the pan.

2. Add the maple syrup, oil, ginger, salt, and pepper. Mix well. Cook, stirring, over medium heat for 5 minutes or until the sauce coats the carrots. Remove from the heat. Serve warm.

Reintroduce Milk: Replace the olive oil with 1 tablespoon butter.

Reintroduce Wheat or Soy: Add 1 tablespoon soy sauce or tamari in step 2.

Reintroduce Sesame: Serve the carrots with 2 teaspoons sesame seeds.

Reintroduce Fish or Shellfish: Serve the carrots with a piece of fish (page 60) or shellfish as the main course.

Per Serving

Calories: 91; Total fat: 4g; Carbohydrates: 15g; Fiber: 3g; Protein: 1g

TERIYAKI GREEN BEANS

SERVES 4

PREP TIME: **10 MINUTES**   COOK TIME: **10 MINUTES**

These green beans get just the right amount of sticky caramelization from cooking and are a luscious treat. Yes, I just used "luscious" to describe a vegetable!

2 tablespoons canola oil

1 teaspoon minced garlic

1 pound green beans, trimmed

2 tablespoons sriracha

1 tablespoon honey

1 teaspoon ground ginger

1. In a large pan or skillet, heat the oil and garlic over medium heat until the oil is shimmering.

2. Add the green beans, sriracha, honey, and ginger. Cook for 7 to 10 minutes or until the green beans are tender but crisp. Remove from the heat. Serve warm.

Reintroduce Wheat or Soy: In place of the sriracha, use 2 tablespoons soy sauce.

Reintroduce Soy: In place of the green beans, use 1 pound edamame.

Reintroduce Peanuts: Sprinkle the green beans with 2 tablespoons crushed peanuts before serving.

Reintroduce Tree Nuts: Sprinkle the green beans with 2 tablespoons sliced almonds or chopped nuts such as pecans or walnuts.

Reintroduce Sesame: Sprinkle the green beans with 2 teaspoons sesame seeds.

Reintroduce Fish or Shellfish: Serve the green beans with a piece of fish (page 60) or shellfish as the main course.

Per Serving

Calories: 116; Total fat: 7g; Carbohydrates: 13g; Fiber: 3g; Protein: 2g

GRILLED VEGETABLES WITH BALSAMIC VINEGAR

SERVES 4

PREP TIME: **10 MINUTES**   COOK TIME: **20 MINUTES**

Foil packets are the best way to cook on the grill because you get the grilled flavor without any of the messy cleanup. This way, you also don't have to worry about using skewers or having half of your vegetables stick to the grill or be burnt to a crisp.

1 small bunch asparagus, woody ends removed

1 red bell pepper, sliced

1 orange bell pepper, sliced

1 zucchini, halved and cut into strips

¼ cup balsamic vinegar

¼ cup olive oil

1 teaspoon table salt

1. Preheat the grill on medium heat.

2. Create 4 boats out of foil by folding up each side of 4 (4-inch square) pieces of foil and pinching the corners together.

3. In a large bowl, combine the asparagus, red bell pepper, orange bell pepper, zucchini, vinegar, oil, and salt. Divide among the foil boats.

4. Put the boats on the grill and cook for 20 minutes or until the vegetables are just tender. Remove from the heat.

Reintroduce Milk: Serve the vegetables with fresh mozzarella cheese.

Reintroduce Fish or Shellfish: Serve the vegetables with a piece of fish (page 60) or shellfish as the main course.

Per Serving

Calories: 173; Total fat: 14g; Carbohydrates: 11g; Fiber: 3g; Protein: 2g

ROASTED TRI-COLOR VEGETABLES

SERVES 4

PREP TIME: **20 MINUTES**   COOK TIME: **45 MINUTES**

This recipe calls for tri-color vegetables, but the more colors, the merrier! Feel free to use any root vegetables in this recipe. Potatoes get all the attention, but there are also parsnips, turnips, yams, beets, rutabaga, and carrots to choose from.

8 ounces beets, cut into 1-inch dice

8 ounces sweet potato, cut into 1-inch dice

8 ounces purple potatoes, cut into 1-inch dice

3 tablespoons olive oil

1 tablespoon dried thyme

1 tablespoon dried rosemary

1 teaspoon table salt

1. Preheat the oven 400°F. Line a baking sheet with parchment paper.

2. Spread the beets, sweet potato, and potatoes out in a single layer on the prepared baking sheet.

3. Drizzle the vegetables with the oil. Sprinkle with the thyme, rosemary, and salt.

4. Transfer the baking sheet to the oven and bake for 35 to 45 minutes or until the edges are crispy (watching carefully to prevent burning). Remove from the oven. Let the vegetables cool for 5 minutes before serving.

Reintroduce Milk: Serve the vegetables with a sour cream or yogurt dip.

Reintroduce Eggs: Serve the vegetables with spicy aïoli (page 107).

Reintroduce Soy: Serve the vegetables with a yogurt dip made from soy yogurt.

Reintroduce Fish or Shellfish: Serve the vegetables with a piece of fish (page 60) or shellfish as the main course.

Per Serving

Calories: 211; Total fat: 10g; Carbohydrates: 28g; Fiber: 5g; Protein: 3g

SIMPLE OVEN FRIES

SERVES 4

PREP TIME: **15 MINUTES**   COOK TIME: **40 MINUTES**

I think everyone has their favorite kind of French fries, whether they're shoestring, steak, crinkle cut, curly, floppy, or crispy. I like my fries crispy on the outside and creamy on the inside, which is what this recipe yields.

1½ pounds Russet potatoes or Yukon Gold potatoes, cut into 1-inch-thick fries

3 tablespoons canola oil

1 teaspoon table salt

1. Preheat the oven 425°F. Line a baking sheet with parchment paper.

2. Pat the potatoes dry and put them in a large bowl with the oil and salt. Toss until evenly coated. Spread out in a single layer on the prepared baking sheet.

3. Transfer the baking sheet to the oven and bake for 30 to 40 minutes or until the edges are crispy (watching carefully to prevent burning). Remove from the oven. Let the fries cool for 5 minutes before serving.

Reintroduce Milk: Serve the fries with a sour cream or yogurt dip or melt ¼ cup shredded cheese over the top to make cheese fries.

Reintroduce Eggs: Serve the fries with spicy aïoli (page 107).

Reintroduce Soy: Serve the fries with a yogurt dip made from soy yogurt.

Reintroduce Fish or Shellfish: Serve the fries with a piece of fish (page 60) or shellfish as the main course.

Per Serving

Calories: 227; Total fat: 11g; Carbohydrates: 31g; Fiber: 2g; Protein: 4g

CORN BREAD

PREP TIME: **10 MINUTES**   COOK TIME: **25 MINUTES**

Corn bread goes beautifully with seafood, soups, chilis, stews, and bar-becue. It also makes for a tasty grab-and-go breakfast.

Nonstick cooking spray, for coating the baking dish

1 cup cornmeal

1 cup gluten-free 1-to-1 flour

½ cup sugar

1 tablespoon baking powder

¼ teaspoon table salt

1 cup plain, unsweetened rice milk

⅓ cup canola oil

1 teaspoon apple cider vinegar

1. Preheat the oven to 400°F. Spray a 9-inch square baking dish with cooking spray.

2. In a large bowl, whisk together the cornmeal, flour, sugar, baking powder, and salt.

3. In a second bowl, whisk together the rice milk, oil, and vinegar.

4. Pour the wet ingredients into the dry ingredients and mix until no lumps or dry spots remain. Pour into the prepared baking dish.

5. Transfer the baking dish to the oven and bake for 20 to 25 minutes or until the edges are golden and a toothpick inserted into the center of the bread comes out clean. Remove from the oven. Cut into squares and serve.

Reintroduce Milk, Soy, or Tree Nuts: In place of the rice milk, use 1 cup milk; plain, unsweetened soy milk; or plain, unsweetened nut milk.

Reintroduce Eggs: In place of the vinegar and baking powder, use 1 egg.

Reintroduce Wheat: In place of the gluten-free flour, use 1 cup all-purpose flour.

Reintroduce Fish or Shellfish: Serve the bread with a piece of fish (page 60) or shellfish as the main course.

Per Serving (1 square)

Calories: 263; Total fat: 10g; Carbohydrates: 41g; Fiber: 1g; Protein: 2g

STREET CORN

SERVES 4

PREP TIME: **5 MINUTES,**
plus 30 minutes to marinate

COOK TIME: **10 TO 15 MINUTES**

Street food is a worldwide favorite for its convenience, reasonable price, variety, and simple deliciousness. Mexican-style street corn (or elote) is a cob of sweet corn covered in savory and spicy sauces and seasonings.

4 ears corn

¼ cup freshly squeezed lime juice

2 tablespoons canola oil

1 teaspoon paprika

1 teaspoon chili powder

½ teaspoon table salt

⅛ teaspoon cayenne pepper

1. In a large bowl, combine the corn, lime juice, oil, paprika, chili powder, salt, and cayenne pepper. Marinate for 30 minutes.

2. Preheat the grill on medium heat.

3. Put the corn on the grill and cook for 10 to 15 minutes; turn often to prevent burning and baste with the marinade at each turn. Remove from the heat. Serve warm.

Reintroduce Milk: Spread 1 tablespoon sour cream on each ear of corn or sprinkle with 1 tablespoon Cotija cheese.

Reintroduce Eggs: Spread 1 tablespoon mayonnaise on each ear of corn.

Reintroduce Tree Nuts: Serve each ear sprinkled with ½ tablespoon crushed pine nuts.

Reintroduce Fish or Shellfish: Serve the corn with a piece of fish (page 60) or shellfish as the main course.

Per Serving

Calories: 192; Total fat: 9g; Carbohydrates: 29g; Fiber: 4g; Protein: 5g

STUFFED MUSHROOMS

SERVES 4

PREP TIME: **15 MINUTES**   COOK TIME: **20 MINUTES**

A stuffed mushroom is like a little boat of happiness. It's a velvety shell that's perfectly customizable with a wide variety of fillings.

4 portabella mushroom caps, cleaned

2 tablespoons olive oil, divided

½ cup thawed frozen spinach

2 tablespoons roasted red peppers

2 tablespoons sun-dried tomatoes

1 tablespoon minced garlic

1 tablespoon lemon juice

½ teaspoon table salt

1. Preheat the oven to 375°F. Line a baking sheet with parchment paper.

2. Brush the inside and outside of each mushroom cap with 1 tablespoon of oil. Arrange in a single layer on the prepared baking sheet.

3. To make the filling, in a medium bowl, combine the spinach, red peppers, sun-dried tomatoes, garlic, lemon juice, salt, and the remaining 1 tablespoon of oil. Divide evenly among the mushroom caps.

4. Transfer the baking sheet to the oven and bake for 20 minutes or until the filling is heated through and the mushroom is tender. Remove from the oven. Serve warm.

Reintroduce Milk: Add ¼ cup grated parmesan cheese in step 3.

Reintroduce Eggs: Serve the mushrooms with simple aïoli (page 101).

Reintroduce Wheat: Add ¼ cup bread crumbs in step 3.

Reintroduce Fish or Shellfish: Serve the mushrooms with a piece of fish (page 60) or shellfish as the main course.

Per Serving

Calories: 94; Total fat: 7g; Carbohydrates: 6g; Fiber: 2g; Protein: 3g

BROCCOLI SLAW

SERVES 4

PREP TIME: **10 MINUTES**

Broccoli slaw is a fun, heartier version of coleslaw that gets a crispy crunch from the broccoli stems. This is also the perfect recipe to reduce food waste because often the thick stalk of the broccoli head goes straight into the trash.

2 large broccoli crowns

2 carrots

1 apple, cored and cut into ½-inch dice

1 cup unsweetened dried cranberries

¼ cup red-wine vinegar

¼ cup olive oil

2 teaspoons onion powder

¼ teaspoon freshly ground black pepper

1. Cut the florets off the heads of broccoli, chop them into bite-size pieces, and put them in a large bowl.

2. Grate the broccoli stems and the carrots over the bowl.

3. Add the apple, cranberries, vinegar, oil, onion powder, and pepper. Toss together until well incorporated. Serve chilled.

Reintroduce Milk: Add ½ cup shredded Cheddar cheese in step 3.

Reintroduce Eggs: In place of the olive oil, use ¼ cup mayonnaise.

Reintroduce Tree Nuts: Add ½ cup chopped walnuts in step 3.

Reintroduce Fish or Shellfish: Serve the slaw with a piece of fish (page 60) or shellfish as the main course.

Per Serving

Calories: 307; Total fat: 15g; Carbohydrates: 45g; Fiber: 8g; Protein: 5g

"BURNT" BROCCOLI CROWNS AND CAULIFLOWER

SERVES 4

PREP TIME: **5 MINUTES**   COOK TIME: **30 MINUTES**

"Burnt" broccoli is a different way of preparing a vegetable that is typically steamed or eaten raw. Roasting the broccoli in the oven until the florets are slightly charred gives the broccoli a nutty flavor that pairs deliciously with any dish.

1 large head broccoli, cut into bite-size pieces

1 large head cauliflower, cut into bite-size pieces

2 tablespoons olive oil

½ teaspoon table salt

½ teaspoon freshly ground black pepper

1. Preheat the oven to 400°F. Line a baking sheet with parchment paper.

2. Place the broccoli and cauliflower on the prepared baking sheet in a single layer. Drizzle with the oil. Season with the salt and pepper.

3. Transfer the baking sheet to the oven and bake for 30 minutes or until deeply browned, checking to prevent burning. Remove from the oven.

Reintroduce Milk: Sprinkle the vegetables with shredded cheese before serving.

Reintroduce Eggs: Serve the vegetables with simple aïoli (page 101).

Reintroduce Fish or Shellfish: Serve the vegetables with a piece of fish (page 60) or shellfish as the main course.

Per Serving

Calories: 122; Total fat: 7g; Carbohydrates: 12g; Fiber: 5g; Protein: 5g

CARAMELIZED BRUSSELS SPROUTS

SERVES 4

PREP TIME: **5 MINUTES**   COOK TIME: **30 MINUTES**

Brussels sprouts are a food that many people claim to hate, but I believe this is because they're so often poorly cooked. When they are cut into small pieces and roasted, the sprouts become crunchy and sweet, making them irresistible. The smaller the sprouts, the better!

1 pound Brussels sprouts, quartered

2 tablespoons olive oil

1 tablespoon lemon juice

½ teaspoon table salt

½ teaspoon freshly ground black pepper

1. Preheat the oven to 400°F. Line a baking sheet with foil.
2. Spread the Brussels sprouts out in a single layer on the prepared baking sheet.
3. Drizzle the Brussels sprouts with the oil and lemon juice. Season with the salt and pepper.
4. Transfer the baking sheet to the oven and bake, checking to prevent burning, for 30 minutes or until the edges are browned. Remove from the oven.

Reintroduce Fish or Shellfish: Serve the Brussels sprouts with a piece of fish (page 60) or shellfish as the main course.

Per Serving

Calories: 109; Total fat: 7g; Carbohydrates: 10g; Fiber: 4g; Protein: 4g

PEACH SORBET 160

SWEETS AND SNACKS

PEACH SORBET

PREP TIME: **5 MINUTES**

The beautiful thing about sorbet is that it is a dairy-free alternative to ice cream and is basically a frozen smoothie. So, if you would make a smoothie with an ingredient, decrease the amount of liquid and you magically have sorbet! You can make large batches of sorbet to keep in the freezer for a refreshing and nutritious treat.

2 cups frozen peaches

2 bananas, peeled

1 teaspoon ground ginger

* In a blender or food processor, combine the peaches, bananas, and ginger. Blend on high speed for 30 to 60 seconds or until no lumps remain. Serve immediately or freeze.

Reintroduce Milk or Soy: Add ½ cup milk or soy milk.

Reintroduce Tree Nuts: Add ½ cup almond milk or serve with candied pecans.

Per Serving (½ cup)

Calories: 56; Total fat: 0g; Carbohydrates: 14g; Fiber: 2g; Protein: 1g

VEGGIE CHIPS

PREP TIME: **15 MINUTES**   COOK TIME: **20 MINUTES**

This is a basic recipe for veggie chips that can be customized however you like. Season these chips with spices, like cumin and chili powder, and a squeeze of lemon juice or with garlic and onion. Or eat them just as they are.

1 pound sweet potatoes

1 pound white potatoes

1 pound beets

3 tablespoons olive oil

½ teaspoon table salt

¼ teaspoon freshly ground black pepper

1. Preheat the oven to 375°F. Line a baking sheet with parchment paper.

2. Using a mandoline or a very sharp knife, shave the sweet potatoes, white potatoes, and beets into very thin slices. Lay as many as you can in a single layer on the prepared baking sheet. Drizzle with the oil. Season with the salt and pepper.

3. Transfer the baking sheet to the oven and bake for 20 minutes, flipping halfway through or until the veggies are golden brown and crispy, like chips. Remove from the oven. Let cool before serving.

Reintroduce Milk: Serve the chips with a sour cream or yogurt dip.

Reintroduce Eggs: Serve the chips with spicy aïoli (page 107).

Reintroduce Soy: Serve the chips with a yogurt dip made from soy yogurt.

Reintroduce Fish or Shellfish: Serve the chips with a piece of fish (page 60) or shellfish as the main course.

Per Serving (1 cup)

Calories: 323; Total fat: 10g; Carbohydrates: 53g; Fiber: 9g; Protein: 6g

POPCORN WITH FLAVOR MIX-INS

PREP TIME: **5 MINUTES**   COOK TIME: **5 MINUTES**

Popcorn isn't just for the movies anymore, and you don't need to load it up with unhealthy butter and salt. Topped with the seasonings of your choice, this healthy snack staple will never grow old.

2 tablespoons olive oil   **½ cup popcorn kernels**

Salsa en Polvo Mix-In

1 tablespoon chili powder   **¼ teaspoon table salt**

1 tablespoon grated lime zest

Ranch Mix-In

½ teaspoon dried dill weed   **½ teaspoon garlic powder**

½ teaspoon dried chives   **½ teaspoon onion powder**

Hot Cocoa Mix-In

1 tablespoon unsweetened   **1 teaspoon sugar**
cocoa powder   **½ teaspoon ground cinnamon**

Churro Mix-In

1 tablespoon ground cinnamon   **1 teaspoon sugar**

1. In a large stockpot, heat the oil over medium heat until shimmering.
2. Add the popcorn and cover. The kernels will pop for 4 minutes. Listen closely: when the popping slows to only every few seconds, your popcorn is done.
3. While hot, toss the popcorn in your choice of seasonings for 10 seconds and serve.

Reintroduce Milk: Add ½ cup milk chocolate chips.

Reintroduce Peanuts or Tree Nuts: Add ½ cup peanuts or tree nuts.

Per Serving Salsa en Polvo (2 cups)

Calories: 73; Total fat: 2g; Carbohydrates: 14g; Fiber: 3g; Protein: 2g

Per Serving Ranch (2 cups)

Calories: 71; Total fat: 2g; Carbohydrates: 13g; Fiber: 3g; Protein: 2g

Per Serving Hot Cocoa (2 cups)

Calories: 74; Total fat: 2g; Carbohydrates: 14g; Fiber: 3g; Protein: 2g

Per Serving Churro (2 cups)

Calories: 74; Total fat: 2g; Carbohydrates: 14g; Fiber: 3g; Protein: 2g

CANDIED DRIED FRUIT

PREP TIME: **5 MINUTES**   COOK TIME: **5 MINUTES**

Traditionally, making candied fruit required knowledge of sugar temperatures and the use of a candy thermometer. This recipe takes a lot of the guesswork out of it by using prediced fruit, simplifying the candying process.

¾ cup water

¼ cup honey

2 cups dried fruit of your choice

2 tablespoons sugar

1. In a large pot, bring the water and honey to a low boil over medium-high heat. Remove from the heat.

2. Add the dried fruit and mix. Soak in the sugar water for 5 minutes.

3. Using a slotted spoon, remove the dried fruit from the pot and transfer to a cooling or drying rack.

4. Sprinkle the dried fruit with the sugar. Once cool, store in an airtight container.

Reintroduce Milk or Soy: Serve the candied fruit with yogurt or soy yogurt.

Reintroduce Peanuts or Tree Nuts: Serve the candied fruit with peanuts, tree nuts, or almond-milk yogurt.

Per Serving (½ cup)

Calories: 245; Total fat: 0g; Carbohydrates: 64g; Fiber: 5g; Protein: 2g

CRISPY RICE CEREAL TREATS

PREP TIME: **10 MINUTES**   COOK TIME: **10 MINUTES**

A crispy rice treat out of a cellophane wrapper is tasty, but a warm, homemade crispy rice treat is out of this world. The best part is that these are allergen-free.

3 tablespoons canola oil

10 to 12 ounces marshmallows, any size

6 cups dry gluten-free rice cereal

1. In a stockpot, warm the oil over low heat. Line a 9-by-13-inch baking dish with parchment paper or wax paper.

2. Add the marshmallows to the pot to melt them. Stir frequently to prevent burning. Remove from the heat.

3. Stir the cereal into the pot.

4. Fill the prepared baking dish with the cereal mixture and press down into all corners, making a flat top to the bars. Let cool for 5 to 10 minutes, then cut into 2-inch squares.

Reintroduce Milk: In place of the oil, use 3 tablespoons butter, or add ½ cup milk chocolate chips.

Reintroduce Wheat: In place of the gluten-free rice cereal, use 6 cups wheat cereal.

Reintroduce Peanuts or Tree Nuts: Add ½ cup peanuts or tree nuts.

Per Serving (1 bar)

Calories: 80; Total fat: 2g; Carbohydrates: 16g; Fiber: 0g; Protein: 1g

YOUR FAVORITE CEREAL BARS

PREP TIME: **10 MINUTES**   COOK TIME: **10 MINUTES**

Cereal bars make a great grab-and-go snack option. This quick-and-easy version does away with any allergy-triggering ingredients.

3 tablespoons canola oil

10 to 12 ounces marshmallows, any size

¼ cup vegan semisweet chocolate chips (check to make sure they are soy-free)

½ cup chopped golden raisins

6 cups dry gluten-free cereal

1. In a stockpot, warm the oil over low heat.
2. Add the marshmallows and chocolate to melt them. Stir frequently to prevent burning. Remove from the heat.
3. Stir in the raisins and cereal.
4. Line a 9-by-13-inch baking dish with parchment paper or wax paper.
5. Fill the prepared baking dish with the cereal mixture and press down into all corners, making a flat top to the bars. Let cool for 5 to 10 minutes, then cut into 2-inch squares.

Reintroduce Milk: Substitute 3 tablespoons butter for the oil or substitute ¼ cup milk chocolate chips for the vegan chocolate chips.

Reintroduce Wheat: Use 6 cups wheat cereal.

Reintroduce Peanuts: Add ½ cup peanuts.

Reintroduce Tree Nuts: Add ½ cup tree nuts.

Per Serving

Calories: 80; Total fat: 2g; Carbohydrates: 16g; Fiber: 0g; Protein: 1g

OATMEAL COOKIES

PREP TIME: **15 MINUTES**   COOK TIME: **10 MINUTES**

There is just something so comforting about an oatmeal cookie. This recipe omits the perpetually joked-about raisins for a classic, chewy, and not-too-sweet oatmeal cookie.

½ **cup gluten-free 1-to-1 flour**	**1 cup rolled oats**
¼ **cup sugar**	¼ **cup vegetable oil or canola oil**
1 teaspoon ground cinnamon	¼ **cup unsweetened applesauce**
½ **teaspoon baking soda**	**1 teaspoon vanilla extract**

1. Preheat the oven to 375°F. Line a baking sheet with parchment paper.

2. In a large bowl, whisk together the flour, sugar, cinnamon, and baking soda until evenly distributed.

3. Add the oats, oil, applesauce, and vanilla. Mix until the oats are evenly coated.

4. Make each cookie from 2 tablespoons of the batter, rolling into a ball and then lightly pressing flat. Arrange on the prepared baking sheet at least 1 inch apart.

5. Transfer the baking sheet to the oven and bake for 10 minutes or until the cookies are golden brown. Remove from the oven. Let them rest on the baking sheet for 5 to 10 minutes to firm up. Serve warm or store for later.

Reintroduce Milk: In place of the oil, use 4 tablespoons butter.

Reintroduce Eggs: In place of the applesauce, use 1 beaten egg.

Reintroduce Wheat: In place of the gluten-free flour, use ½ cup all-purpose flour.

Reintroduce Peanuts or Tree Nuts: Add ½ cup peanuts or tree nuts.

Per Serving (1 cookie)

Calories: 71; Total fat: 3g; Carbohydrates: 10g; Fiber: 1g; Protein: 1g

CHOCOLATE CHIP COOKIES

MAKES 36 COOKIES

PREP TIME: **20 MINUTES**   COOK TIME: **15 TO 18 MINUTES**

This is a big deal. I am making public my personal recipe for the best chocolate chip cookies in the world. Enjoy them, guilt-free.

2 cups gluten-free 1-to-1 flour

½ cup granulated sugar

½ cup light or dark brown sugar

1 teaspoon baking soda

1 teaspoon table salt

½ teaspoon baking powder

¾ cup canola oil

½ cup unsweetened cherry applesauce

2 teaspoons vanilla extract

1 cup vegan chocolate chips (check to make sure they are soy-free)

1. Preheat the oven to 350°F. In a large bowl, whisk together the flour, granulated sugar, brown sugar, baking soda, salt, and baking powder.

2. In a small bowl, whisk together the oil, applesauce, and vanilla.

3. To make the dough, add the wet ingredients to the dry ingredients, folding together thoroughly. Add the chocolate chips and mix until evenly distributed.

4. Scoop 1 tablespoon of the dough per cookie onto the prepared baking sheet, leaving some room between each piece of dough. Flatten gently with the back of a spoon.

5. Transfer the baking sheet to the oven and bake the cookies for 15 to 18 minutes, depending on whether you like them gooey or firmer. Remove from the oven. Eat them warm.

Reintroduce Milk: In place of the vegan chocolate chips, use milk chocolate chips.

Reintroduce Eggs: In place of the applesauce, use 2 eggs.

Reintroduce Wheat: In place of the gluten-free flour, use all-purpose flour.

Reintroduce Peanuts or Tree Nuts: Add ½ cup peanuts or tree nuts in step 3.

Per Serving (1 cookie)

Calories: 121; Total fat: 6g; Carbohydrates: 16g; Fiber: 0g; Protein: 0g

SAVORY CEREAL MIX

MAKES 4 CUPS

PREP TIME: **5 MINUTES**   COOK TIME: **5 MINUTES**

Warm homemade cereal mix is light-years tastier than a bag you can buy in the snack aisle at the grocery store. Even better, this version is free of the top 9 allergens.

2 cups corn square cereal, like Chex

2 cups rice square cereal, like Chex

2 tablespoons olive oil

1 teaspoon paprika

1 teaspoon garlic powder

1 teaspoon onion powder

½ teaspoon ground red pepper

1. In a large, microwave-safe bowl, toss together the corn cereal, rice cereal, oil, paprika, garlic powder, onion powder, and red pepper until well incorporated.
2. Microwave on high for 2½ minutes, stir, then microwave for 2½ more minutes.
3. Let cool for 10 minutes and serve.

Reintroduce Milk: Add 2 tablespoons butter.

Reintroduce Wheat or Soy: Add ¼ cup Worcestershire sauce.

Reintroduce Wheat: In place of 2 cups of either cereal, use wheat square cereal (like Chex) or toasted O's cereal (like Cheerios).

Reintroduce Peanuts or Tree Nuts: Add ½ cup peanuts or tree nuts in step 1.

Per Serving (½ cup)

Calories: 87; Total fat: 4g; Carbohydrates: 13g; Fiber: 0g; Protein: 1g

SUNFLOWER SEED BUTTER AND CHOCOLATE CEREAL MIX

MAKES 5 CUPS

PREP TIME: **5 MINUTES**   COOK TIME: **5 MINUTES,**
plus 30 minutes to cool

This cereal mix makes for the perfect late-night treat or party snack. Chocolate has a soul mate in salty, crunchy ingredients, and believe it or not, you can enjoy the flavor of chocolate while avoiding milk.

¼ cup sunflower seed butter

½ tablespoon cocoa powder

1 teaspoon vanilla extract

¼ teaspoon table salt

5 cups rice square cereal or corn square cereal, like Chex

1 cup powdered sugar

1. In a large, microwave-safe bowl, combine the sunflower seed butter, cocoa powder, vanilla, and salt. Microwave for 30 seconds, stir, then microwave for 30 more seconds or until the ingredients have melted together.

2. Gently fold in the cereal.

3. Add the sugar and toss until all squares are coated. Refrigerate for 30 minutes before serving.

Reintroduce Milk: Add 2 tablespoons melted butter in step 1.

Reintroduce Wheat: In place of 2 cups of the rice cereal or corn cereal, use wheat square cereal.

Reintroduce Peanuts or Tree Nuts: In place of the sunflower seed butter, use peanut butter or almond butter.

Per Serving (½ cup)

Calories: 135; Total fat: 4g; Carbohydrates: 24g; Fiber: 1g; Protein: 2g

NO-BAKE CHOCOLATE BITES

PREP TIME: **45 MINUTES**

These no-bake bites are the perfect treat for dessert or anytime you're craving something sweet. Make a double or triple batch that you can store in the freezer.

¾ **cup rolled oats**

¾ **cup sunflower seed butter**

¼ **cup unsweetened cocoa powder**

1 **teaspoon vanilla extract**

¼ **cup vegan dark chocolate chips, 60 to 85 percent (check to make sure they are soy-free)**

1. In a blender, combine the oats, sunflower seed butter, cocoa powder, and vanilla. Puree for 30 seconds or until a thick paste is made. Transfer to a large bowl.

2. Add the chocolate chips and stir to combine.

3. Make each bite using 2 tablespoons of the mixture. Roll into balls and arrange in a single layer on a plate. Freeze for 30 minutes. Store in an airtight container in the refrigerator.

Reintroduce Milk: In place of the dark chocolate, use milk chocolate chips.

Reintroduce Peanuts or Tree Nuts: In place of the sunflower seed butter, use peanut butter or almond butter.

Per Serving (1 bite)

Calories: 51; Total fat: 4g; Carbohydrates: 3g; Fiber: 1g; Protein: 2g

GUACAMOLE AND SALSA

SERVES 4

PREP TIME: **15 MINUTES**   COOK TIME: **10 MINUTES**

This classic snack has a little bit of everything: whole grains, fruits, vegetables, fiber, healthy fat, vitamins, minerals, and antioxidants.

16 (6-inch) corn tortillas

2 tablespoons olive oil

1 tablespoon smoked paprika

2 ripe medium avocados, pitted, peeled, and diced

1 medium white onion, finely diced, divided

3 large hothouse tomatoes, diced, divided

1 jalapeño, finely diced, divided

1 lime, halved

1 tablespoon minced garlic

1. Preheat the oven to 350°F. Line a baking sheet with parchment paper.

2. While the oven is preheating, brush the tortillas with the oil and sprinkle evenly with the paprika. Cut into quarters. Arrange in a single layer on the prepared baking sheet or as closely to a single layer as your pan size will allow.

3. Transfer the baking sheet to the oven and bake for 10 minutes or until the tortilla pieces begin to brown. The chips may feel soft but will crisp further as they cool. Remove from the oven.

4. While the chips are cooking, begin preparing the guacamole and salsa. In a medium bowl, mash the avocados until mostly smooth.

5. Mix in half of the onion, 1 diced tomato, and half of the jalapeño.

6. In a blender or food processor, combine the remaining 2 diced tomatoes, onion, jalapeño, the juice of half of the lime, and the garlic. Blend to the desired consistency. Pour into a bowl.

7. Once the chips are done baking, squeeze the remaining lime juice over them. Let cool for 10 minutes and serve with dips.

Reintroduce Milk or Eggs: In step 6, add ½ cup sour cream or ¼ cup mayonnaise.

Per Serving

Calories: 520; Total fat: 25g; Carbohydrates: 71g; Fiber: 17g; Protein: 11g

ROASTED CHICKPEAS

MAKES ABOUT 2 CUPS

PREP TIME: **5 MINUTES**   COOK TIME: **45 MINUTES**

Rich in protein, roasted chickpeas are a perfect snack but also work as a crouton substitute on a salad or as a crunchy soup topping. Make sure to dry the chickpeas well and thoroughly coat with olive oil to reach maximum crunchiness.

1 (15-ounce) can chickpeas, drained, rinsed, and blotted dry

1 tablespoon olive oil

¼ teaspoon chili powder

¼ teaspoon garlic powder

1. Preheat the oven to 450°F. Line a baking sheet with parchment paper.
2. In a large bowl, toss the dried chickpeas in the oil for 10 seconds.
3. Spread the chickpeas out in a single layer on the prepared baking sheet.
4. Transfer the baking sheet to the oven and roast for 45 minutes or until the chickpeas are golden brown, checking after 30 minutes and monitoring closely to prevent burning. Remove from the oven. Let cool for 10 minutes.
5. In a bowl, toss the chickpeas with the chili powder and garlic powder and serve.

Reintroduce Eggs: Drizzle the chickpeas with simple aïoli (page 101).

Per Serving (½ cup)

Calories: 110; Total fat: 5g; Carbohydrates: 13g; Fiber: 4g; Protein: 4g

HUMMUS

MAKES ABOUT 2 CUPS

PREP TIME: **10 MINUTES**   COOK TIME: **20 MINUTES**

Hummus is a relatively blank canvas that can be flavored just about any way you like. Add roasted red peppers for a smoky-flavored hummus; avocado for a guacamole-like dip with the added benefit of protein; or pumpkin puree or sweet potato with cumin, chili powder, and chipotle pepper for a spicy-sweet variation.

1 (15-ounce) can chickpeas, drained and rinsed

2 cups water

¼ teaspoon baking soda

⅓ cup plain, unsweetened sunflower seed butter

2 tablespoons lemon juice

2 tablespoons ice cold water

1 teaspoon minced garlic

1 tablespoon olive oil

1. In a medium saucepan, cover the chickpeas with the water.

2. Add the baking soda. Bring to a boil over high heat. Cook for 20 minutes or until the skins are falling off. Remove from the heat. Drain and rinse.

3. In a blender or food processor, combine the chickpeas, sunflower seed butter, lemon juice, water, and garlic. Blend for 2 to 3 minutes or until creamy and smooth.

4. Serve the hummus in a bowl with the oil drizzled on top.

Reintroduce Sesame: In place of the sunflower seed butter, use tahini.

Reintroduce Peanuts or Tree Nuts: In place of the sunflower seed butter, use plain, unsweetened peanut butter or almond butter.

Per Serving (2 tablespoons)

Calories: 60; Total fat: 4g; Carbohydrates: 5g; Fiber: 1g; Protein: 2g

SUNFLOWER SEED BUTTER CUPS

PREP TIME: **5 MINUTES,**
plus overnight to freeze

Three ingredients and a freezer are all you need for this creamy, luscious, salty, and sweet treat.

1½ **cups sunflower seed butter**

**6 tablespoons fruit preserves of
  your choice**

½ **teaspoon table salt**

1. Line a 6-cup cupcake tin with cupcake liners.
2. Scoop 2 tablespoons of sunflower seed butter into the bottom of each well, flattening with the back of a spoon to reach all edges.
3. Scoop 1 tablespoon of preserves into the center of each well.
4. Cover the preserves with 2 tablespoons of sunflower seed butter per well, smoothing to reach all edges.
5. Sprinkle the cups with the salt. Freeze overnight and enjoy!

Reintroduce Milk: Melt 2 cups milk chocolate chips to dip the cups in halfway through freezing.

Reintroduce Peanuts or Tree Nuts: In place of the sunflower seed butter, use peanut butter or almond butter.

Per Serving (1 cup)

Calories: 450; Total fat: 35g; Carbohydrates: 29g; Fiber: 4g; Protein: 11g

SAMPLE FOOD TRACKER

When using an elimination diet as a tool to discover your trigger foods, staying organized will reduce your stress. Getting into the good habit of writing down what you eat throughout the day will save the guesswork and help you pinpoint what food caused symptoms. This is a sample food tracker, but feel free to use any method that keeps you organized, such as notes on your phone or computer or a small notebook you carry around. Italicized words are examples of what you might write in.

Meal	Food/Drink	Symptoms	Changes
Breakfast Reintroduction Day 1: Dairy	*Light 'n' Fluffy Pancakes (replaced the rice milk with 1 cup of milk)* *1 cup of coffee with sugar* *1 glass of water*	*Did not notice any symptoms from the added milk*	*Never had issues with pancakes before*
Lunch Reintroduction Day 1: Dairy	*Kale Chopped Salad (added ¼ cup of shredded parmesan cheese)* *1 glass of iced tea with lemon*	*Did not notice any symptoms from the parmesan cheese*	*Never had issues with hard cheeses like parmesan before*
Dinner Reintroduction Day 1: Dairy	*Beef Enchilada Casserole (added ½ cup of shredded Monterey Jack cheese)* *1 glass of water*	*Stomachache started about an hour after dinner; feeling gassy and crampy*	*Have noticed these symptoms with melted cheese before*
Snack/Dessert Reintroduction Day 1: Dairy	*Peach Sorbet (added ½ cup of milk)*	*Stomachache is even worse; had some diarrhea overnight*	*Have noticed these symptoms with ice cream before, and having just had dairy for dinner and dairy for dessert exacerbated my symptoms*

MEASUREMENT CONVERSIONS

	US Standard	US Standard (Ounces)	Metric (Approximate)
VOLUME EQUIVALENTS (LIQUID)	2 tablespoons	1 fl. oz.	30 mL
	¼ cup	2 fl. oz.	60 mL
	½ cup	4 fl. oz.	120 mL
	1 cup	8 fl. oz.	240 mL
	1½ cups	12 fl. oz.	355 mL
	2 cups or 1 pint	16 fl. oz.	475 mL
	4 cups or 1 quart	32 fl. oz.	1 L
	1 gallon	128 fl. oz.	4 L
VOLUME EQUIVALENTS (DRY)	⅛ teaspoon	——————	0.5 mL
	¼ teaspoon	——————	1 mL
	½ teaspoon	——————	2 mL
	¾ teaspoon	——————	4 mL
	1 teaspoon	——————	5 mL
	1 tablespoon	——————	15 mL
	¼ cup	——————	59 mL
	⅓ cup	——————	79 mL
	½ cup	——————	118 mL
	⅔ cup	——————	156 mL
	¾ cup	——————	177 mL
	1 cup	——————	235 mL
	2 cups or 1 pint	——————	475 mL
	3 cups	——————	700 mL
	4 cups or 1 quart	——————	1 L
	½ gallon	——————	2 L
	1 gallon	——————	4 L
WEIGHT EQUIVALENTS	½ ounce	——————	15 g
	1 ounce	——————	30 g
	2 ounces	——————	60 g
	4 ounces	——————	115 g
	8 ounces	——————	225 g
	12 ounces	——————	340 g
	16 ounces or 1 pound	——————	455 g

	Fahrenheit (F)	Celsius (C) (Approximate)
OVEN TEMPERATURES	250°F	120°C
	300°F	150°C
	325°F	180°C
	375°F	190°C
	400°F	200°C
	425°F	220°C
	450°F	230°C

INDEX FOR ALLERGEN REINTRODUCTION

INDEX

INDEX

ACKNOWLEDGMENTS

*To my husband, who pushed me
to write every day, and to my daughter
whose cuddles and smiles made it
even more worthwhile.*

*Thank you to the wonderful team
at Callisto for all your hard work.
It has been an absolute pleasure
working with you all.*

Amanda Foote, RD, is a registered dietitian, author, proud fire wife, and mother. She runs her own virtual nutrition practice, Amanda Foote Nutrition, specializing in food allergies and intolerance and special (therapeutic) diets for medical conditions that require following a specific diet. It is her calling to ensure that food remains an enjoyable, nourishing part of the human experience, despite dietary restrictions.

Amanda has worked as a registered dietitian for InnovAge and the South Adams County Fire Department and is currently running her nutrition practice. Amanda has a bachelor's degree in dietetics from the University of Northern Colorado and a bachelor's degree in applied psychology from Regis University.

Amanda lives in Colorado with her family and pets. In her spare time, she enjoys developing new recipes, sketching, crafting, reading, biking, and all things Disney.

CPSIA information can be obtained
at www.ICGtesting.com
Printed in the USA
BVHW022331071120
592708BV00003BA/3